SEAFOOD DIET COOKBOOK

How to Cook All Types of Seafood in All Types of Ways

(Best-ever Yummy Quick Seafood Dinner Cookbook for Beginners)

Sally Hughes

Published by Alex Howard

© **Sally Hughes**

All Rights Reserved

Seafood Diet Cookbook: How to Cook All Types of Seafood in All Types of Ways (Best-ever Yummy Quick Seafood Dinner Cookbook for Beginners)

ISBN 978-1-990169-86-1

All rights reserved. No part of this guide may be reproduced in any form without permission in writing from the publisher except in the case of brief quotations embodied in critical articles or reviews.

Legal & Disclaimer

The information contained in this book is not designed to replace or take the place of any form of medicine or professional medical advice. The information in this book has been provided for educational and entertainment purposes only.

The information contained in this book has been compiled from sources deemed reliable, and it is accurate to the best of the Author's knowledge; however, the Author cannot guarantee its accuracy and validity and cannot be held liable for any errors or omissions. Changes are periodically made to this book. You must consult your doctor or get professional medical advice before using any of the suggested remedies, techniques, or information in this book.

Table of contents

Part 1 1

How to Properly Cook Shrimp 9

25 Delicious Shrimp Recipes 16

(1) Easy Shrimp Salad 17

(2) Tasty Louisiana Style Shrimp and Grits 18

(3) Delicious Seafood Style Chowder 20

(4) Peppered Shrimp Alfredo 22

(5) Chipotle Spiced Shrimp Tacos 24

(6) Delicious Marinated Grilled Shrimp 26

(7) Margarita Style Grilled Shrimp 28

(8) Hearty Bacon Wrapped BBQ Shrimp 30

(9) Healthy Asparagus and Shrimp 31

(10) Louisiana Style Creole Shrimp 33

(11) Creamy Pesto Smothered Shrimp 35

(12) Shrimp Packed Fried Rice 37

(13) Cajun Style Shrimp Soup 39

(14) Traditional Cioppino 41

(15) Walnut and Honey Spiced Shrimp 43

(16) Champagne Smothered Shrimp and Pasta 45

(17) Szechwan Style Shrimp 48

(18) Shrimp and Feta Smothered Pasta 50

(19) Angel Hair Pasta Tossed with Fresh Basil and Shrimp .. 52

(20) Happy Style Shrimp 54

(21) Slow Cooker Style Jambalaya 56

(22) Tasty Shrimp and Mushroom Linguini Smothered in a Cream Cheese Herb Sauce 58

(23) Classic Shrimp Scampi Bake 60

(24) Cajun Style Seafood Pasta 62

(25) Coconut Style Shrimp 64

Part 2 66

Honey Garlic Salmon 67

Maryland Crab Cakes 69

Roast Cod with Garlic Butter 71

Balsamic Glazed Salmon 73

Caribbean Sea Bass 75

Bacon-Wrapped Scallops 77

Tuna Patties Recipe 78

Lemon and Garlic Tilapia (Baked) with Mango Salsa 80

Baked fish 82

Stewed Fried Fish 84

Seafood Lasagna 86

Grilled Seafood Packs with Lemon-Chive Butter 89

Conch Fritters 91

Bubba's Crab Stew	92
Lobster Mac and Cheese	93
Perfectly Seared Scallops	96
Shrimp Fried Rice	98
Calamari Fritti with Pepperoncini Aioli	100
Stuffed Mushrooms	102
Grace Shrimp Curry	104
Barbecued Fish Rolls	105
Baked Fish with Yam Stuffing	106
Brown Fish Stew	107
Zuppa di Pesce (seafood soup)	110
Crespoline Cosimo	111
Conch Pie or Conch Stew	113
Salmon Filet with Mango Cilantro Salsa	115
Grilled Maple Mustard Salmon	116
Cape Mudge Halibut Chowder	117
Baked Halibut With Tarragon Crust	118
Steamed Fish	119
Sea Trout Salad	121
Scrambled Fish	123
Baked Crab Guadeloupe-Style	124
Caribbean-Style Crabs	126
Fish Loaf	127

Thai-Dyed Seafood Soup 128

Lobster Eggs Benedict With Crispy Potato Pancakes & Bearnaise Sauce 129

Tamarind Shrimp 132

Sour And Hot Fish 133

Chile Prawns 134

Costa Rican Tilapia 136

Roatan Honduras Conch Soup 138

Almond Tree Snapper with Lemon Herbed Butter 139

Beer Batter Fish 141

Crab Chowder with Sherry 142

Antigua Scallop and King Prawns Salad 143

Shrimp Pie 145

Shrimp Moqueca 146

Shrimp Cuscuz 147

Corn And Shrimp Soup 148

SALADS 149

Easy Nicoise Salad Recipe 149

Fennel and Shrimp Salad Recipe 151

Lemon Mustard with Thyme Dressing: 151

Mediterranean Chicken Salad Recipe 153

Tuna, Egg and Potato Salad Recipe 155

Honey Lemon Mustard Dressing: 156

Spiral Pasta and Tuna Salad with Olives Recipe 157
Fresh Summer Fruit Salad 159
SNACKS 160
Cucumber and Carrot Sticks in Ranch Dip 160
Tomato and Herb Bruschetta 162
Veggies with Garlic Hummus 163
Pita Chips and Veggies with Hummus 165
Hummus 166
Yogurt Cereal and Berry Parfait 167
RISOTTOS 169
Creamy Asparagus Risotto with Parmesan 169
Easy Seafood Risotto 171
Pumpkin and Sage Risotto 173
Risotto with Spinach and Parmesan 175
Easy Vegetarian Risotto 178
Easy Risotto with Salmon and Zucchini 180
SEAFOOD 182
Asian Pan Fried Cod with Spring Onions Recipe 182
Homemade Chili Garlic Prawns Recipe 184
Asian-Style Shrimp and Vegetable Sauté Recipe 186
Breaded Fish Fillet Recipe 188
Grilled Scallops with Teriyaki Sauce Recipe 190

Part 1

(1) Can Help Fight Against Cancer

Shrimp contains a key component known as carotenoids which can help fight against the various types of cancers that you can obtain throughout your life. Shrimp also contains a product known as selenium which has always been connected to reducing the levels of cancer within the body such as lung and prostate cancer.

This is because these components contain key antioxidant enzymes which help fight against the presence and effects of free radicals which have been known to cause cancer in the past. On top of that these components also help to boost the immune system so that your body can fight off these cancer cells on its own.

(2) Can Help You to Lose Weight

Shrimp is an excellent source of both protein and Vitamin D. Best of all shrimp is packed full of these nutrients without having you intake any carbohydrates in the process, making shrimp the best ingredient to use in your cooking if you are looking to lose weight.

By consuming shrimp, you will also receive a sufficient amount of zinc which can increase the levels of leptin in the body which is a natural hormone use to regulate the body's appetite and fat storage. By increasing these hormone levels in your body naturally, you can help to prevent common weight gaining issues such as over eating and bothersome food cravings.

On top of that shrimp contains high levels of iodine which can also help to control how much energy your body uses while you are resting. This can even help you to lose more weight and prevent gaining weight in the process.

(3) Can Help Prevent Cardiovascular Disease

If you are the type of person that currently has heart disease that runs within your family, then enjoying shrimp may be the perfect solution for you. Shrimp contains an enzyme that can help break up blood clots within the body's blood vessels.

On top of that shrimp contains high levels of Omega 3 fatty acids which can also help eliminate dangerous levels of cholesterol within the bloodstream and help to prevent heart attacks and strokes in the future.

(4) Help to Promote Healthy Brain Health

Shrimp itself is known for its high levels of iron which your body needs to help transfer oxygen to your red blood cells. When you add additional iron into your body you can increase the oxygen flow that is occurring throughout your body to your muscles and to other essential organs which can not only provide strength, but also help increase endurance. On top of that the increase in oxygen can help to improve your brain as well such as improving your memory and improving your concentration.

(5) Contains Anti-Aging Properties

One of the most common causes of aging today is the sun outside. Without proper sunlight protection people are more prone to developing wrinkles, age spot and even severe cases of sunburn.

When you add shrimp to your daily diet you can help prevent these aging properties from occurring and can help get rid of years of age from your face. On top of that shrimp itself contains high levels of a compound known as astazanthin which is a strong antioxidant that can help reduce any signs of aging as your grow older.

With that said if you are very concerned with aging and your appearance, then adding shrimp to your diet at least once or twice a week is something that you may be interested in.

(6) Promote Healthy Bone Health

Shrimp is packed full of protein and various vitamins that your body needs to help fight against bone degeneration such as calcium phosphorous and magnesium. When you have a deficiency in these types of essential proteins and vitamins that you need for your bones to stay healthy, you will lose overall bone mass and strength in the process. This can lead to dangerous diseases such as osteoporosis which is a weakening of your bone structure. To increase the fight against bone degeneration it is a great idea to add shrimp to your diet on a weekly basis to keep you feeling stronger in the long run.

(7) Can Help Prevent Hair Loss

The various minerals that you can find in shrimp today and help to prevent hair loss in the future. Hair loss ca sometimes be caused by a zinc deficiency and plays a huge role in maintain current hair cells. This can help those who are starting to lose their hair and can help promote healthy hair growth as well.

How to Properly Cook Shrimp

One thing about shrimp that you need to understand is that most people tend to cook it for way too long. Cooking shrimp is not as complicated as it seems to be, but it is something that is not for the average novice chef. The reason why people cook shrimp is because of its versatility, sweetness and how fast it can be prepared. However, there are a few mistakes that you want to avoid making and there are proper ways to cook shrimp correctly. In this section, you will learn how to cook shrimp the right way and avoid some of these mistakes in the process.

(1) Use the Freshest Shrimp Possible

You would be surprised how perishable fresh shrimp can be. When you purchase shrimp, it is ideal that you cook them within 24 hours of getting them because they perish that quickly. Regardless if you are using fresh shrimp, you want to make sure that you buy it frozen with the shells on and purchase the wild-caught variety.

If you are unsure if your shrimp is too old to cook, give it a smell. If it smells like ammonia you need to toss them out because they are too old to use.

(2) Always Defrost Your Shrimp Before Cooking

Once you have your shrimp you want to make sure that you always defrost it before you cook it. When you try to cook still frozen shrimp especially in hot water you can risk cooking your shrimp unevenly. The best and simplest way to defrost the shrimp is to put them in a bowl filled with cold water while the water is running in the process. Doing it this way will have your shrimp defrosted in a matter of minutes.

(3) Devein Your Shrimp the Proper Way

When it comes to deveining, this is something that people tend to mess up on all of the time. What ends up happening is that while they are trying to devein the shrimp they also mingle it in the process. The best way to devein your shrimp is to use a sharp knife or kitchen shears which helps to give you the best ways of shelling your shrimp and for cleaning all the gross stuff out. You need to keep in mind that shrimp are incredibly delicate so it is always best to handle them for as least amount of time as possible.

(4) Save The Heads and The Shells

Once people devein and deshell their shrimp most of the time they end up throwing the heads and shells out. However, one thing that many people do not realize is that the heads of the shrimp as well as their shells are packed full of the shrimp flavor that you know and love. The best thing that you can do in this case is to conserve the shrimp heads and shells into a freezer bag and then cook them later on with some butter and a dash of salt. Either way they are going to taste great.

(5) Always Season Your Shrimp

Another common mistake that many people tend to make when making shrimp is not seasoning the shrimp. The best type of shrimp is always filled with a sweet and oceanic flavor but they are also tender as well. You want to add to that flavor by seasoning it with your favorite types of seasoning. However, you need to keep in mind that the best type of seasoning to use is always the most simple such as an Old Bay Seasoning or a simple dash of salt and pepper.

(6) Don't Overcook Your Shrimp

This is a struggle that many people tend to have, myself included. When it comes to making shrimp, there is a general rule that you should follow.

- Straight shaped shrimp is an indicator that your shrimp is under cooked.
- When you have shrimp that is curled into a C shape, this lets you know that your shrimp has been cooked to perfection.
- When you have shrimp that is in the shape of an O, they are overcooked and cannot be repaired.

25 Delicious Shrimp Recipes

(1) Easy Shrimp Salad

If you are looking for a delicious dish to bring along with you to your next family picnic, this is one dish you are going to want to make for yourself. It is so delicious I guarantee your entire family will be begging you for the recipe.

Serving Size: 6 Servings

Cooking Time: 15 Minutes

Ingredient List

- 1 Pound of Shrimp, Large in Size, Peeled, Deveined and Fully Cooked
- 1 Cup of Celery, Fresh and Roughly Chopped
- 1 Carrot, Large in Size and Finely Shredded
- ½ Cup of Onions, Finely Chopped
- 2 Eggs, Large in Size, Hard Boiled and Finely Chopped
- ¾ Cup of Mayonnaise, Your Favorite Kind
- Dash of Salt and Pepper, For Taste

Instructions:

1. Use a large sized bowl and add in all of your ingredients.

2. Season your dish with a dash of salt and pepper and stir thoroughly to combine.

3. Cover with a sheet of plastic wrap and set into your fridge to chill until you are ready to serve it.

(2) Tasty Louisiana Style Shrimp and Grits

Here is a country style shrimp recipe I know that is going to leave your mouth watering for more. Best of all this dish is incredibly easy to make and is packed full of a delicious flavor I know you won't be able to resist.

Serving Size: 2 Servings

Cooking Time: 40 Minutes

Ingredient List

- 1 Cup of Water, Warm
- Dash of Salt, For Taste
- 6 Tablespoon of Grits, Your Favorite Kind
- 2 Tablespoon of Olive Oil, Extra Virgin Variety
- ½ Cup of Ham, Tasso Variety and Finely Diced
- 2 Tablespoon of Bell Pepper, Green in Color
- 20 Shrimp, Medium in Size, Peeled and Deveined
- ¼ Cup of Wine, White in Color
- 1 Cup of Whipping Cream, Heavy Variety
- Dash of Salt and Pepper, For Taste
- 1 Tablespoon of Green Onions, Finely Chopped and Fresh

Instructions:

1. The first thing that you will want to do is bring your water and your dash of salt into a small sized saucepan.

Set over medium heat and add in your grits. Stir thoroughly until evenly mixed. Once boiling reduce the heat to low and allow your grits to simmer until they are tender to the touch. This should take at least 20 minutes. After this time remove and set aside for later use.

2. Next heat up some oil in a large sized skillet placed over medium to high heat. Once your oil is hot enough add in your ham and cook until crispy to the touch.

3. After this time add in your onions and chopped bell pepper. Cook for the next 4 minutes or until your onions are translucent.

4. Add in your shrimp into this mixture with at least another spoonful of your oil. Cook for the next 30 to 45 seconds or until your shrimp turns pink in color. Remove your mixture from your skillet and set aside for later use.

5. Pour your wine into your skillet and deglaze your pan completely. Once deglazed add in your heavy cream and reduce the heat to low. Allow your mixture to simmer for the next 10 minutes or until thick in consistency. Season with a dash of salt and pepper.

6. Serve your grits and top off with your shrimp. Pour your sauce over the top and garnished with your green onions. Serve right away and enjoy.

(3) Delicious Seafood Style Chowder

If you are looking for a delicious and filling dish to enjoy on a cold winter's night, then this is the perfect dish for you to make. Feel free to add in your favorite ingredients for the tastiest results.

Serving Size: 8 Servings

Cooking Time: 1 Hour

Ingredient List

- 1 ½ Cups of Milk, Fat Free Variety
- 1, 8 Ounce Can of Cream Cheese, Fat Free Variety
- 2 Cloves of Garlic, Minced
- 1, 26 Ounce Can of Cream of Mushroom Soup, Fat Free and Condensed Variety
- 1 Cup of Green Onions, Fresh and Roughly Chopped
- 1 Cup of Carrots, Thinly Sliced
- 1, 15.25 Ounce Can of Corn, Whole Kernel Variety and Undrained
- 1 ½ Cups of Potatoes, Finely Chopped
- 1 teaspoon of Parsley, Fresh and Dried
- ½ teaspoon of Black Pepper, For Taste
- ½ teaspoon of Cayenne Pepper, For Taste
- ½ Pound of Shrimp
- ½ Pound of Scallops, Bay Variety
- ½ Pound of Crab Meat, Fresh

- ½ Pound of Calamari, Cut into Tubes
- 1, 6.5 Ounce Can of Claims, Canned Variety and Finely Chopped

Instructions:

1. Place at least half a cup of your milk, soft cream cheese and minced garlic into a large sized pot placed over low heat. Cook for at least 5 minutes.

2. Then add in your condensed soup, fresh green onions, fresh carrots, corn along with the liquid accompanied with it, diced potatoes, fresh parsley and your remaining milk. Stir thoroughly to combine and season with a dash of pepper and cayenne pepper.

3. Allow your mixture to simmer for the next 25 minutes.

4. After this time add in your shrimp, bay style scallops, fresh crabmeat, tubes of calamari and clams. Continue to cook for the next 10 minutes.

5. Discard any clams that do not open on their own accord and remove from heat. Serve while still piping hot and enjoy.

(4) Peppered Shrimp Alfredo

If you are a huge fan of alfredo dishes, then this is the perfect dish for you to make. This delicious shrimp recipe is smothered in a creamy alfredo sauce and topped off with hearty Portobello mushrooms and peppers, making for a delicious dish to enjoy whenever you wish.

Serving Size: 6 Servings

Cooking Time: 50 Minutes

Ingredient List

- 12 Ounces of Pasta, Penne Variety
- ¼ Cup of Butter, Soft
- 2 Tablespoon of Olive Oil, Extra Virgin Variety
- 1 Onion, Medium in Size and Finely Diced
- 2 Cloves of Garlic, Minced
- 1 Bell Pepper, Red in Color and Finely Diced
- ½ Pound of Mushrooms, Portobello Variety and Finely Diced
- 1 Pound of Shrimp, Medium in Size, Peeled and Deveined
- 1, 15 Ounce Jar of Alfredo Sauce, Your Favorite Kind
- ½ Cup of Romano Cheese, Freshly Grated
- ½ Cup of Cream, Heavy Whipping Variety
- 1 teaspoon of Cayenne Pepper, For Taste
- Dash of Salt and Pepper, For Taste

- ¼ Cup of Parsley, Roughly Chopped and Fresh

Instructions:

1. First bring a large sized pot of water to a boil over medium heat. Once your water is boiling add in your pasta and cook for the next 8 to 10 minutes or until tender to the touch. Drain your pasta after this time and set aside for later use.

2. While your pasta is cooking add your butter and oil into a large sized saucepan placed over medium heat. Once your oil and butter is hot enough add in your onions and cook until soft to the touch. This should take at least 2 minutes.

3. After this time add in your minced garlic, diced pepper and mushrooms. Continue to cook over medium to high heat until your mixture is tender to the touch. This should take at least 2 to 3 minutes.

4. After this time add in your shrimp and continue to cook until pink in color and firm to the touch. Add in your favorite kind of alfredo sauce, grated cheese and heavy cream. Stir thoroughly to combine and allow to simmer for the next 5 minutes or until thick in consistency.

5. Season your dish with a dash of salt and black pepper followed by a dash of cayenne pepper.

6. Add in your drained pasta and stir to coat thoroughly.

7. Serve with a garnish of your fresh parsley and enjoy right away.

(5) Chipotle Spiced Shrimp Tacos

If you are a huge fan of classic tacos, but love the taste of shrimp, then this is the perfect dish for you to make. Smothered in spicy chipotle taste and garnished with some fresh cilantro, even the pickiest of eaters will love this dish.

Serving Size: 6 Servings

Cooking Time: 30 Minutes

Ingredient List

- 1, 12 Ounce Pack of Bacon, Cut into Small Sized Pieces
- ½ of an Onion, Finely Diced
- 2 Pounds of Shrimp, Large in Size, Peeled, Fully Cooked and Cut IN Half
- 3 Peppers, Chipotle Variety, In Adobo Sauce and Minced
- 12 Tortillas, Corn Variety
- 1 Cup of Cilantro, Fresh and Roughly Chopped
- 1 Lime, Fresh and Juice Only
- Dash of Salt, For Taste and Optional

Instructions:

1. Use a large sized deep skillet and add in your bacon. Cook over medium to high heat until your bacon is brown in color. Drain your excess bacon fat.

2. Add in your onions and cook for another 5 minutes or until the onions are translucent.

3. Then add in your shrimp and pepper. Continue to cook for another 4 minutes or until piping hot.

4. Next heat up your corn tortillas in a large sized skillet placed over medium to high heat for at least 10 to 15 minutes.

5. Fill your hot tortillas with your cooked shrimp mixture. Top off with your fresh cilantro, fresh lime juice and dash of salt. Serve right away and enjoy.

(6) Delicious Marinated Grilled Shrimp

This is a very simple yet delicious shrimp recipe to make whenever you are looking for a delicious grilled meal to enjoy. This dish is packed full of a spicy taste that I know you won't be able to get enough.

Serving Size: 6 Servings

Cooking Time: 55 Minutes

Ingredient List

- 3 Cloves of Garlic, Minced
- 1/3 Cup of Olive Oil, Extra Virgin Variety
- ¼ Cup of Tomato Sauce
- 2 Tablespoon of Vinegar, Red Wine Variety
- 2 Tablespoon of Basil, Fresh and Roughly Chopped
- ½ teaspoon of Salt, For Taste
- ¼ teaspoon of Cayenne Pepper
- 2 Pounds of Shrimp, Fresh, Peeled and Deveined

Instructions:

1. Use a large sized bowl and add in your minced garlic, olive oil, tomato sauce and vinegar. Stir thoroughly to combine.

2. Season this mixture with your fresh basil, dash of salt and cayenne pepper.

3. Add your fresh shrimp into this mixture and toss until thoroughly coated.

4. Cover this bowl with some plastic wrap. Place into your fridge to chill for the next 30 minutes to an hour, making sure to stir once or twice during the marinating process.

5. While your shrimp is marinating preheat your grill to medium heat.

6. Place your marinated shrimp onto metallic skewers. Toss out the rest of your marinade.

7. Place your shrimp onto your grill and cook for at least 2 to 3 minutes on each side or until your shrimp is opaque in color. Remove and serve while still piping hot.

(7) Margarita Style Grilled Shrimp

Here is yet another delicious grilled shrimp recipe I know you are going to want to make during your next family cookout. For the tastiest results, I highly recommend marinating your shrimp for at least 3 hours before grilling.

Serving Size: 4 Servings

Cooking Time: 50 Minutes

Ingredient List

- 1 Pound of Shrimp, Peeled and Deveined
- 3 Tablespoon of Olive Oil, Extra Virgin Variety
- 3 Tablespoon of Cilantro, Fresh and Roughly Chopped
- 2 Tablespoon of Lime Juice, Fresh
- 2 Cloves of Garlic, Minced
- 2 teaspoon of Tequila, Your Favorite Kind
- ¼ teaspoon of Cayenne Pepper, For Taste
- ¼ teaspoon of Salt, For Taste
- 4 Skewers, Bamboo Variety and Soaked

Instructions:

1. The first thing that you will want to do is place your shrimp, dash of salt and cayenne pepper, fresh lime juice, fresh cilantro and olive oil in a large sized bowl. Cover your bowl with some plastic wrap and place into

your fridge to marinate for at least 30 minutes to 3 hours.

2. After this time preheat an outdoor grill to high heat. Lightly grease the grate of your grill with a generous amount of oil.

3. Place your marinated shrimp onto your skewers and place onto your grill. Grill for the next 2 to 3 minutes on each side of until your shrimp turns pink in color. Remove and serve while still piping hot. Enjoy!

(8) Hearty Bacon Wrapped BBQ Shrimp

These delicious bacons wrapped shrimp is not only spicy to taste, but packed full of a shrimp flavor nobody in your home will be able to resist for long. Feel free to serve this dish as a hearty entrée or an appetizer.

Serving Size: 3 Servings

Cooking Time: 50 Minutes

Ingredient List

- 16 Shrimp, Large in Size, Peeled and Deveined
- 8 Slices of Bacon, Thick Cut
- Some Barbecue Seasoning, Your Favorite Kind and For Taste

Instructions:

1. The first thing that you will want to do is preheat your oven to 450 degrees.

2. While your oven is heating up wrap at least half a slice of bacon around a piece of shrimp. Secure in place using a toothpick and repeat until all of your shrimp has been wrapped.

3. Season your shrimp with your barbecue seasoning and allow to sit on a large sized greased baking sheet for the next 15 minutes.

4. After this time place your shrimp into your oven to bake for the next 10 to 15 minutes. After this time remove and allow to cool slightly before serving.

(9) Healthy Asparagus and Shrimp

If you are looking for a healthy yet incredibly delicious dish to make, then this is the perfect dish for you to make. Tossed with filling egg noodles and healthy asparagus, this is one dish you won't have to feel guilty about enjoying.

Serving Size: 8 Servings

Cooking Time: 50 Minutes

Ingredient List

- 1 Pound of Asparagus, Fresh
- 1, 16 Ounce Pack of Egg Noodles
- 4 Cloves of Garlic, Minced
- ½ Cup of Olive Oil, Extra Virgin Variety
- 1 Cup of Butter, Soft
- 1 Tablespoon of Lemon Juice, Fresh
- 1 Pound of Shrimp, Medium in Size, Peeled and Deveined
- 1 Pound of Mushrooms, Fresh and Sliced Thinly
- ½ Cup of Parmesan Cheese, Freshly Grated
- Dash of Salt and Pepper, For Taste

Instructions:

1. Using a small sized saucepan boil your asparagus with enough water to cover it until your asparagus is

tender to the touch. Once tender roughly chop and set aside for later use.

2. Then bring a large sized pot of water over medium heat. Bring to a boil and season your water with a dash of salt. Once boiling add in your pasta. Cook until tender to the touch. This should take at least 8 to 10 minutes. Once tender, remove, drain and set aside for later use.

3. After this time use a large sized saucepan and add in your oil. Set over low to medium heat and cook until your garlic is golden brown in color.

4. After this time add in your butter and fresh lemon juice. Cook until your butter is fully melted and add in your shrimp. Cook until your shrimp begins to turn pink in color before adding in your thin mushrooms and tender asparagus. Continue to cook until your mushrooms are tender to the touch.

5. Remove from heat and add in your cooked egg noodles. Toss thoroughly to combine and serve with a topping of freshly grated Parmesan cheese.

(10) Louisiana Style Creole Shrimp

Here is yet another southern style dish I know you are going to love making. Packed full of fresh tomatoes, shrimp, garlic and onions, this is a classic Louisiana style dish that can be made as a main entrée or as a side dish. Either way it will taste amazing.

Serving Size: 5 Servings

Cooking Time: 45 Minutes

Ingredient List

- ½ Cup of Onion, Finely Diced
- ½ Cup of Bell Pepper, Green in Color and Finely Chopped
- ½ Cup of Celery, Finely Chopped and Fresh
- 2 Cloves of Garlic, Minced
- 3 Tablespoon of Butter, Soft
- 2 Tablespoon of Cornstarch
- 1, 14.5 Ounce Can of Tomatoes, Stewed Variety
- 1, 8 Ounce Can of Tomato Sauce
- 1 Tablespoon of Worcestershire Sauce
- 1 teaspoon of Chili, Powdered Variety
- Dash of Hot Sauce, Your Favorite Kind
- 1 Pound of Shrimp, Medium in Size, Peeled and Deveined

Instructions:

1. Use a medium sized saucepan and add in your butter. Set over medium heat and once your butter is melted add in your diced onions, bell pepper, fresh celery and minced garlic. Stir to combine and cook until tender to the touch.

2. Add in your cornstarch, diced tomatoes, tomato sauce, Worcestershire sauce, powdered chili and hot sauce. Stir to combine and bring your mixture to a boil.

3. Once your mixture is boiling add in your shrimp and allow to cook for the next 5 minutes. After this time remove from heat and serve while still piping hot.

(11) Creamy Pesto Smothered Shrimp

If you are looking for a healthy shrimp recipe to enjoy, then this is the perfect recipe for you to enjoy. It is packed full of Italian taste that I know you won't be able to get enough of. Feel free to substitute your shrimp with some crab. Regardless it will taste delicious.

Serving Size: 8 Servings

Cooking Time: 30 Minutes

Ingredient List

- 1 Pound of Pasta, Linguine Variety
- ½ Cup of Butter, Soft
- 2 Cups of Cream, Heavy Variety
- ½ teaspoon of Black Pepper, For Taste
- 1 Cup of Parmesan Cheese, Freshly Grated
- 1/3 Cup of Pesto, Homemade Variety
- 1 Pound of Shrimp, Large in Size, Peeled and Deveined

Instructions:

1. Bring a large sized pot of water over medium heat. Bring to a boil and season with a dash of salt and once your water is boiling add in your pasta. Cook for the next 8 to 10 minutes or until tender to the touch. Once tender to the touch remove and drain. Set your pasta aside for later use.

2. Next heat up some butter in a large sized skillet placed over medium heat. Once your butter is fully melted add in your heavy cream and season with a dash of pepper for taste. Cook for the next 6 to 8 minutes, making sure to stir thoroughly during this time.

3. Add in your grated Parmesan cheese and stir thoroughly until fully incorporated. Add in your pesto and continue to cook for the next 3 to 5 minutes or until thick in consistency.

4. After this time add in your shrimp and cook for the next 5 minutes or until your shrimp turns pink in color.

5. Remove from heat and serve over your cooked linguine.

(12) Shrimp Packed Fried Rice

If you love the taste of classic fried rice, then this is the perfect dish for you to make. Serve this fried rice with your favorite Chinese or Japanese dish to make a filling meal that you won't be able to get enough of.

Serving Size: 4 Servings

Cooking Time: 30 Minutes

Ingredient List

- 1 ½ Cups of White Rice, Uncooked
- 3 Cups of Water, Warm
- 4 Tablespoon of Oil, Vegetable Variety
- 1 Cup of Bean Sprouts, Fresh
- ½ Cup of Onions, Finely Chopped
- 1 ½ Cups of Shrimp, Medium in Size, Peeled and Deveined
- ¼ Cup of Green Onions, Fresh and Roughly Chopped
- 2 Eggs, Large in Size and Beaten
- 1 teaspoon of Salt, For Taste
- ¼ teaspoon of Black Pepper, For Taste
- 4 Tablespoon of Soy Sauce, Your Favorite Kind
- ¼ teaspoon of Oil, Sesame Variety

Instructions:

1. Use a large sized saucepan and add in your water. Bring it to a boil over medium heat before adding in

your rice. Stir thoroughly and cover. Reduce the heat to low and then allow to simmer for the next 20 minutes or until fully cooked through. Once fully cooked set your rice aside to cool completely.

2. Then heat up a large sized skillet over medium heat for at least 2 minutes. Once your skillet is hot to the touch add in your oil, fresh bean sprouts and finely chopped onions. Stir well to combine and cook for the next 3 minutes.

3. Add in your cooled rice along with your shrimp. Cook for the next 3 minutes, making sure to stir thoroughly during this time.

4. After this time add in your fresh green onions, large eggs, dash of salt and pepper, favorite kind of soy sauce and sesame style oil. Continue to cook for another 4 to 5 minutes or until your eggs are fully cooked through.

5. Remove from heat and serve right away.

(13) Cajun Style Shrimp Soup

If you are looking for a hearty and filling soup recipe to make during the cold winter months, this is the perfect dish for you to make. It is easy to prepare and makes for a filling dish whenever you are tight on time.

Serving Size: 6 Servings

Cooking Time: 40 Minutes

Ingredient List

- 1 Tablespoon of Butter, Soft
- ½ Cup of Bell Pepper, Green in Color and Finely Chopped
- ¼ Cup of Green Onions, Finely Chopped and Fresh
- 1 Clove of Garlic, Minced
- 3 Cups of Cocktail Juice, Tomato and Vegetable Variety
- 1, 8 Ounce Bottle of Clam Juice, Fresh
- ½ Cup of Water, Warm
- ¼ teaspoon of Thyme, Dried Variety
- ¼ teaspoon of Basil, Dried Variety
- ¼ teaspoon of Red Pepper Flakes, Crushed
- 1 Bay Leaf, Fresh and Dried
- ½ teaspoon of Salt, For Taste
- ½ Cup of White Rice, Uncooked Variety
- ¾ Pound of Shrimp, Peeled and Deveined
- Some Hot Sauce, For Taste

Instructions:

1. Add your butter into a large sized pot placed over medium heat. Once your butter is fully melted add in your bell peppers, onions and minced garlic. Cook until tender to the touch.

2. Once tender add in your veggie juice, fresh clam juice and warm water. Season this mixture with your fresh thyme, fresh basil, crushed red pepper, fresh bay leaf and dash of salt. Stir thoroughly to combine.

3. Bring this mixture to a boil before adding in your rice. Reduce the heat to low and cover. Allow your mixture to simmer for the next 15 minutes or until your rice is tender to the touch.

4. After this time add in your shrimp and continue to cook for another 5 minutes or until your shrimp is opaque.

5. Remove your bay leaf after this time and season with a touch of hot sauce. Enjoy!

(14) Traditional Cioppino

Here is a wonderful seafood style stew recipe I know you won't be able to get enough of. For the tastiest results, I highly recommend serving this dish with some warm and crusty bread for dipping.

Serving Size: 13 Servings

Cooking Time: 55 Minutes

Ingredient List
- ¾ Cup of Butter, Soft
- 2 Onions, Finely Chopped
- 2 Cloves of Garlic, Minced
- 1 Bunch of Parsley, Fresh and Roughly Chopped
- 2, 14.5 Ounce Cans of Tomatoes, Stewed Variety
- 2, 14.5 Ounce Cans of Broth, Chicken and Homemade Preferable
- 2 Bay Leaves, Fresh and Dried
- 1 Tablespoon of Basil, Fresh and Dried
- ½ teaspoon of Thyme, Fresh and Dried
- ½ teaspoon of Oregano, Fresh and Dried
- 1 Cup of Water, Warm
- 1 ½ Cups of Wine, White in Color
- 1 ½ Pounds of Shrimp, Large in Size, Peeled and Deveined
- 1 ½ Pound of Scallops, Bay Variety
- 18 Clams, Small in Size

- 18 Mussels, Cleaned and Debearded
- 1 ½ Cups of Cram Meat, Fresh
- 1 ½ Pounds of Cod, Cut into Fillets and Cut into Small Sized Cubes

Instructions:

1. First place a large sized stockpot over low to medium heat. Add in your butter and once your butter is hot enough add in your chopped onions, minced garlic and fresh parsley. Cook for the next 5 to 7 minutes or until your onions are soft to the touch.

2. Add in your tomatoes after this time along with your homemade broth, fresh bay leaves, fresh basil, fresh thyme, fresh oregano, warm water and wine. Stir thoroughly to mix and cover. Continue to simmer for the next 30 minutes.

3. After this time add in your shrimp, bay scallops, clams, fresh crab meat and mussels. Add in your Cod and stir thoroughly to combine.

4. Bring your mixture to a boil before reducing the heat to low. Allow your mixture to simmer over low heat while covered for the next 5 to 7 minutes or until your clams begin to open. Toss out any of your clams that do not open by themselves.

5. Remove from heat and serve your soup while still piping hot.

(15) Walnut and Honey Spiced Shrimp

Here is a sweet tasting shrimp recipe I know you won't be able to get enough of. This makes crispy shrimp that is smothered in a creamy sauce you will want to make over and over again.

Serving Size: 4 Servings
Cooking Time: 30 Minutes
Ingredient List
- 1 Cup of Water, Warm
- 2/3 Cup of Sugar, White in Color
- ½ Cup of Walnuts, Finely Chopped
- 4 Eggs, Large in Size and Whites Only
- 2/3 Cup of Flour, Rice Variety
- ¼ Cup of Mayonnaise, Your Favorite Kind
- 1 Pound of Shrimp, Large in Size, Peeled and Deveined
- 2 Tablespoon of Honey, Raw
- 1 Tablespoon of Milk, Condensed and Sweetened Variety
- 1 Cup of Oil, Vegetable Variety and For Frying

Instructions:

1. First add your water and white sugar in a small sized saucepan and set over medium heat. Bring your mixture to a boil before adding in your walnuts. Boil

your walnuts for the next 2 minutes before draining. Set aside to dry completely.

2. Add your egg whites into a medium sized bowl and use an electric mixer to beat until foamy in consistency.

3. Add in your rice flour and beat again until a paste begins to form.

4. Then heat up some oil in a large sized skillet placed over medium to high heat. While your oil is heating up dip your shrimp in your rice flour mixture and add into your skillet. Fry for the next 5 minutes or until golden brown in color. Remove and set aside for later use.

5. Use a medium sized bowl and add in your favorite kind of mayonnaise, raw honey and milk. Stir thoroughly to combine and add in your cooked shrimp. Toss to coat and serve with a garnish of your walnuts. Enjoy right away.

(16) Champagne Smothered Shrimp and Pasta

This is yet another delicious pasta dish that I know will become a favorite in your household. This is an elegant dish that you can make whenever you are looking to impress your friends and family.

Serving Size: 4 Servings

Cooking Time: 30 Minutes

Ingredient List

- 8 Ounces of Pasta, Angel Hair Variety
- 1 Tablespoon of Olive Oil, Extra Virgin Variety
- 1 Cup of Mushrooms, Fresh and Thinly Sliced
- 1 Pound of Shrimp, Medium in Size, Peeled and Deveined
- 1 ½ Cups of Champagne, Your Favorite Kind
- ¼ teaspoon of Salt, For Taste
- 2 Tablespoon of Shallots, Minced
- 2 Tomatoes, Plum Variety and Finely Diced
- 1 Cup of Cream, Heavy Variety
- Dash of Salt and Black Pepper, For Taste
- 3 Tablespoon of Parsley, Fresh and Roughly Chopped
- Dash of Parmesan Cheese, Freshly Grated

Instructions:

1. First bring a large sized pot of water seasoned with a dash of salt to a boil over medium heat. Once your water is boiling add in your pasta and cook for the next 8 to 10 minutes or until tender to the touch. Once tender remove, drain and set aside for later use.

2. While your pasta is cooking heat up some oil in a large sized skillet over medium to high heat. Once your oil is hot enough add in your mushrooms and cook for the next 5 to 8 minutes or until tender to the touch. Once tender remove your mushrooms and set aside for later use.

3. Next add in your shrimp, favorite kind of champagne and dash of salt in your skillet. Cook over high heat and bring your mixture to a boil. Once boiling remove your shrimp and set aside for later use.

4. Add your shallots and tomatoes into your champagne mixture. Continue to boil until your mixture is reduced by at least half a cup. This should take at least 8 minutes.

5. Add in at least ¾ cup of your cream and continue to boil for the next 1 to 2 minutes or until slightly thick in consistency.

6. Transfer your shrimp and mushrooms back into your sauce. Season with a dash of salt and pepper and stir to thoroughly combine.

7. Add your fully cooked pasta into a medium sized bowl and add in your remaining ¼ cup of cream and fresh parsley. Toss thoroughly to combine.

8. Serve your pasta with your shrimp mixture over the top. Garnish with your Parmesan cheese and enjoy right away.

(17) Szechwan Style Shrimp

If you are a huge fan of classic Chinese cuisine, then this is the perfect recipe for you to put together. It is incredibly simple to make yet is packed with a spicy and impressive taste that your entire family with love.

Serving Size: 4 Servings

Cooking Time: 20 Minutes

Ingredient List
- 4 Tablespoon of Water, Warm
- 2 Tablespoon of Ketchup, Your Favorite Kind
- 1 Tablespoon of Soy Sauce, Your Favorite Kind
- 2 teaspoon of Cornstarch
- 1 teaspoon of Honey, Raw
- ½ teaspoon of Red Pepper Flakes, Crushed
- ¼ teaspoon of Ginger, Ground Variety
- 1 Tablespoon of Oil, Vegetable Variety
- ¼ Cup of Green Onions, Fresh and Thinly Sliced
- 4 Cloves of Garlic, Minced
- 12 Ounces of Shrimp, Fully Cooked and With Tails Removed

Instructions:

1. Use a medium sized bowl and add in your warm water, favorite kind of ketchup, favorite kind of soy sauce, cornstarch, raw honey, crushed pepper flakes

and ginger. Stir to thoroughly combine and set aside for later use.

2. Heat up some oil in a large sized skillet placed over medium to high heat. Once your oil is hot enough add in your fresh green onions and minced garlic. Cook for the next 30 seconds.

3. After this time add in your shrimp and toss to thoroughly coat.

4. Slowly add in your sauce and cook for the next 5 to 10 minutes or until your sauce is thick in consistency.

5. Remove from heat and serve whenever you are ready.

(18) Shrimp and Feta Smothered Pasta

Here is yet another Italian style dish I know you won't be able to get enough of. This is a great dish to make if you do not have much experience cooking shrimp and if you want to make something more on the elegant side.

Serving Size: 5 Servings

Cooking Time: 30 Minutes

Ingredient List

- 3 Tablespoon of Olive Oil, Extra Virgin Variety
- 1 Pound of Shrimp, Peeled and Deveined
- 5 Cloves of Garlic, Minced
- 1 Tablespoon of White Wine, Your Favorite Kind
- 1 Pound of Pasta, Linguine Variety
- 2 Tomatoes, Finely Chopped
- 1 teaspoon of Oregano, Fresh and Dried
- ½ teaspoon of Basil, Fresh and Dried
- 1, 6 Ounce Pack of Feta Cheese, Crumbled

Instructions:

1. Using a medium sized skillet set over medium heat, add in your oil. Once your oil is hot enough add in your shrimp, minced garlic and favorite wine. Cook for the next 5 minutes or until your shrimp is pink in color. Once pink remove from your skillet and set aside for later use.

2. Next bring a large sized pot of water to a boil over medium heat. Season with a dash of salt and add in your linguine. Cook for the next 8 to 10 minutes or until tender to the touch. Once tender remove, drain and set aside for later use.

3. While your pasta is cooking add in some more oil into your skillet. Once your skillet is hot enough add in your tomatoes, fresh oregano and dried basil. Cook over medium heat and cook until tender to the touch. This should take at least 10 minutes.

4. Remove from heat and add your shrimp and pasta into your skillet. Add in your feta cheese and tomato sauce. Toss to thoroughly to combine and serve whenever you are ready.

(19) Angel Hair Pasta Tossed with Fresh Basil and Shrimp

Here is an easy Italian shrimp dish I know you are going to want to make all of the time. It is incredibly easy to put together and makes for a savory meal to enjoy whenever you want to spoil yourself.

Serving Size: 4 Servings

Cooking Time: 35 Minutes

Ingredient List

- ¼ Cup of Olive Oil, Extra Virgin Variety and Evenly Divided
- 1, 8 Ounce Pack of Pasta, Angel Hair Variety
- 1 teaspoon of Garlic, Finely Chopped
- 1 Pound of Shrimp, Large in Size, Peeled and Deveined
- 2, 28 Ounce Cans of Tomatoes, Italian Style and Drained
- ½ Cup of White Wine, Dried
- ¼ Cup of Parsley, Fresh and Roughly Chopped
- 3 Tablespoon of Basil, Fresh and Roughly Chopped
- 3 Tablespoon of Parmesan Cheese, Freshly Grated

Instructions:

1. The first thing that you will want to do is bring a large sized pot of water to a boil over medium heat.

Add in a tough of oil and add in your pasta. Cook in your boiling water until tender to the touch. Once tender remove, drain and set aside for later use.

2. Next heat up some more oil in a large sized skillet placed over medium heat. Once your oil is hot enough add in your garlic and cook for the next minute or until your garlic is tender to the touch.

3. Add in your shrimp and cook for the next 3 to 5 minutes. Remove your shrimp from your skillet and set aside for later use.

4. Add your chopped tomatoes, dry wine, fresh parsley and fresh basil to your skillet. Stir to thoroughly combine and cook for the next 8 to 12 minutes or until your liquid has been fully reduced.

5. Add your shrimp back into your skillet and continue to cook for another 2 to 3 minutes.

6. After this time remove from heat and serve over a bed of your angel hair pasta. Garnish with some fresh Parmesan cheese and enjoy right away.

(20) Happy Style Shrimp

Just as the name of this dish implies, this is one shrimp dish that will leave you feeling incredibly happy. This dish is smothered in a creamy and spicy shrimp meal that pairs excellently with some crusty bread and a bed of hot pasta.

Serving Size: 4 Servings

Cooking Time: 40 Minutes

Ingredient List
- ¼ Cup of Butter, Soft
- 1 ½ teaspoon of Garlic, Minced
- 1 Pound of Shrimp, Peeled and Deveined
- ¼ Cup of Green Onions, Fresh and Roughly Chopped
- ¼ Cup of White Wine, Dried Variety
- 1/3 Cup of Cream, Heavy Variety
- 2 Tablespoon of Basil, Fresh and Roughly Chopped
- 2 Tomatoes, Roma Variety and Finely Chopped
- Dash of Cayenne Pepper, For Taste
- Dash of Salt and Black Pepper, For Taste

Instructions:

1. The first thing that you will want to do is melt your butter in a large sized skillet placed over medium to high heat. Once your butter is fully melted add in your medium sized shrimp, minced garlic and fresh green

onions. Cook until your shrimp is pink in color. This should take at least 5 minutes.

2. Once your shrimp is cooked remove from your skillet and set aside for later use.

3. Using the same skillet add in your wine, heavy cream, finely diced tomatoes, fresh basil and dash of cayenne pepper. Stir to combine and bring this mixture to a simmer. Once simmering reduce the heat to low and allow to simmer for the next 10 minutes or until slightly thick in consistency.

4. Return your shrimp back into your skillet and toss to coat thoroughly. Season with a dash of salt and pepper. Remove from heat and serve right away.

(21) Slow Cooker Style Jambalaya

If you are a huge fan of classic Southern cooking, then this is one dish I know you are going to love making. For the tastiest results serve this dish over a bed of freshly made hot rice.

Serving Size: 12 Servings

Cooking Time: 8 Hours and 20 Minutes

Ingredient List

- 1 Pound of Chicken Breasts, Boneless, Skinless and Cut into Small Sized Cubes
- 1 Pound of Andouille Sausage, Thinly Sliced
- 1, 28 Ounce Can of Tomatoes, Finely Diced and With Juice
- 1 Onion, Large in Size and Finely Chopped
- 1 Bell Pepper, Green in Color and Finely Chopped
- 1 Cup of Celery, Fresh and Roughly Chopped
- 1 Cup of Chicken Broth, Homemade Preferable
- 2 teaspoon of Oregano, Fresh and Dried
- 2 teaspoon of Parsley, Fresh and Dried
- 2 teaspoon of Cajun Seasoning
- 1 teaspoon of Cayenne Pepper, For Taste
- ½ teaspoon of Thyme, Fresh and Dried
- 1 Pound of Shrimp, Fully Cooked and Without Tails

Instructions:

1. Use a slow cooker and add in your chicken, sausage, fresh tomatoes with their juice, onions, diced pepper, fresh celery and homemade broth. Stir to combine.

2. Season your mixture with your fresh and dried thyme, oregano, parsley, dash of cayenne pepper and your Cajun seasoning. Stir to thoroughly incorporate your seasonings.

3. Cover and cook on the lowest setting for the next 7 to 8 hours or on the highest setting for the next 3 to 4 hours.

4. During the last 30 minutes of cooking add in your shrimp and stir to combine.

5. Turn off your slow cooker after this time and serve your dish while still piping hot.

(22) Tasty Shrimp and Mushroom Linguini Smothered in a Cream Cheese Herb Sauce

If you are looking for the ultimate satisfying dish to serve up, then this is the perfect dish for you to make. It is packed full of shrimp and mushrooms to make a filling and satisfying meal that you will not be able to get enough of.

Serving Size: 4 Servings

Cooking Time: 30 Minutes

Ingredient List

- 1, 8 Ounce Pack of Linguini
- 2 Tablespoon of Butter, Soft
- ½ Pound of Mushrooms, Fresh and Thinly Sliced
- ½ Cup of Butter, Soft
- 2 Cloves of Garlic, Minced
- 1, 3 Ounce Pack of Cream Cheese, Soft
- 2 Tablespoon of Parsley, Fresh and Roughly Chopped
- ¾ teaspoon of Basil, Fresh and Dried
- 2/3 Cup of Water, Boiling
- ½ Pound of Shrimp, Fully Cooked

Instructions:

1. First bring a large sized pot of water to a boil over medium in heat. Season with a dash of salt and add in your linguini. Cook for the next 7 to 9 minutes or until tender to the touch. Once tender remove and drain. Set aside for later use.

2. While your pasta is heat up add your butter into a large sized skillet and set over medium to high heat. Once your butter is fully melted add in your mushrooms. Cook for the next 5 to 10 minutes or until your mushrooms are tender to the touch. Once tender transfer your mushrooms to a plate and set aside for later use.

3. Using the same skillet and in at least half a cup of butter. Once your butter is fully melted and add in your garlic. Cook for at least 30 seconds before adding in your soft cream cheese. Continue to cook until your cream cheese begins to melt.

4. Add in your fresh parsley and fresh basil. Allow to simmer for the next 5 minutes and add in your boiling water. Stir thoroughly until your sauce is smooth in consistency.

5. Add in your fully cooked shrimp and your cooked mushrooms. Continue to cook for the next 2 to 3 minutes or until your sauce is piping hot. Remove from heat.

6. Serve your shrimp sauce on top of a bed of your cooked pasta.

(23) Classic Shrimp Scampi Bake

This is an easy shrimp scampi recipe to make if you are looking for an easy and tasty shrimp recipe to put together in no time. It is so easy to make that you can have this meal ready on your table in just a matter of minutes.

Serving Size: 6 Servings

Cooking Time: 45 Minutes

Ingredient List

- 1 Cup of Butter, Soft
- 2 Tablespoon of Mustard, Dijon Variety and Fully Prepared
- 1 Tablespoon of Lemon Juice, Fresh
- 1 Tablespoon of Garlic, Finely Chopped
- 1 Tablespoon of Parsley, Fresh and Roughly Chopped
- 2 Pounds of Shrimp, Medium in Size, Shelled and Deveined

Instructions:

1. The first thing that you will want to do is preheat your oven to 450 degrees.

2. While your oven is heating up use a small sized saucepan and set over medium heat. Once your saucepan is hot enough add in your soft butter, fresh lemon juice, Dijon mustard, finely chopped garlic and

fresh parsley. Stir thoroughly to combine and continue to cook until your butter is fully melted.

3. Next place your shrimp into the bottom of a medium sized baking dish. Pour your butter mixture over your shrimp.

4. Place into your oven to bake for the next 12 to 15 minutes or until your shrimp is pink in color.

5. Remove after this time and allow to cool slightly before serving.

(24) Cajun Style Seafood Pasta

Here is yet another Italian style pasta recipe I know you won't be able to get enough of. It is somewhat spicy for the taste and packed full of a delicious seafood dish that you will want to make over and over again.

Serving Size: 6 Servings

Cooking Time: 15 Minutes

Ingredient List

- 2 Cups of Cream, Heavy Whipping Variety
- 1 Tablespoon of Basil, Fresh and Roughly Chopped
- 1 Tablespoon of Thyme, Fresh and Roughly Chopped
- 2 teaspoons of Salt, For Taste
- 2 teaspoons of Black Pepper, For Taste
- 1 ½ teaspoon of Red Pepper Flakes, Crushed Variety
- 1 teaspoon of Pepper, White in Color and Ground
- 1 Cup of Green Onions, Fresh and Roughly Chopped
- 1 Cup of Parsley, Fresh and Roughly Chopped
- ½ Pound of Shrimp, Peeled and Deveined
- ½ Pound of Scallops, Bay Variety
- ½ Cup of Swiss Cheese, Finely Shredded
- ½ Cup of Parmesan Cheese, Freshly Grated
- 1 Pound of Pasta, Fettuccine Variety and Dried

Instructions:

1. Bring a large sized pot of water over medium heat. Bring to a boil and season with a dash of salt. Once your mixture is boiling add in your fettucine. Cook for the next 10 to 12 minutes or until tender to the touch. Once tender remove and drain. Set aside for later use.

2. Add your cream into a large sized skillet. Set over medium heat and cook until boiling. Once boiling reduce the heat to low and add in your dash of salt and pepper, chopped basil, chopped thyme, fresh green onions and fresh parsley.

3. Allow your mixture to simmer for the next 7 to 8 minutes or until thick in consistency.

4. Add in your shrimp and bay scallops. Cook until your shrimp is not transparent.

5. Add in your parmesan cheese and shredded swiss cheese. Stir well until evenly blended. Remove from heat.

6. Serve your sauce on top of a bed of fettucine. Enjoy right away.

(25) Coconut Style Shrimp

Here is yet another shrimp recipe I know you are going to love. These tasty shrimps are crispy to the touch and rolled in a coconut beer batter that is going to leave your mouth watering. Feel free to serve this shrimp with your favorite dipping sauce for the tastiest results.

Serving Size: 6 Servings

Cooking Time: 1 Hour

Ingredient List

- 1 Egg, Large in Size and Beaten Lightly
- ½ Cup of Flour, All Purpose Variety
- 2/3 Cup of Beer, Dark in Color and Your Favorite Kind
- 1 ½ teaspoon of Baker's Style Baking Powder
- ¼ Cup of Flour, All Purpose Variety
- 2 Cups of Coconut, Flaked and Lightly Toasted
- 24 Shrimp, Large in Size, Shelled and Deveined
- 3 Cups of Oil, Vegetable Variety and For Frying

Instructions:

1. Use a medium sized bowl and add in your large beaten egg, half a cup of flour, your dark beer and baker's style baking powder. Stir to thoroughly combine.

2. Add your flour into a separate medium sized bowl and add your flaked coconut into another medium sized bowl.

3. First dredge your shrimp in your flour, making sure to shake off the excess flour. Dip into your egg and beer batter and roll in your flaked coconut. Place your coated shrimp onto a large sized baking sheet lined with a sheet of wax paper.

4. Place into your fridge to chill for the next 30 minutes. During this time heat up your oil in a large sized frying pan until piping hot.

5. After this time add in your shrimp and cook for at least 2 to 3 minutes or until golden brown in color. Remove and place onto a plate lined with some paper towels. Serve with your favorite dipping sauce and enjoy.

Part 2

Honey Garlic Salmon

Ingredients
- 1 lb. salmon fillet

Sauce
- 1 teaspoon garlic, minced
- ½ teaspoon ginger, minced
- 4 tablespoons honey
- 2 tablespoons soy sauce

Directions
- Combine the sauce ingredients and marinate the salmon for 15-30 minutes
- Arrange salmon on a foil-lined baking sheet and bake at 350 degrees F for 15-20 minutes depending on thickness, basting the salmon with the sauce halfway through

- Over medium high heat, bring the sauce to a boil and simmer for 3-5 minutes until reduced
- Dish and serve hot drizzled with remaining sauce

NOTES: For a slightly crisp and caramelized top, sear the top of the salmon over medium high heat for 1-2 minutes before baking.

Maryland Crab Cakes

Ingredients

- 1 pound fresh crab meat, picked clean of shells
- 3 tablespoons flour
- 3 tablespoon mayonnaise
- 1 teaspoon dijon mustard
- 1 egg, beaten
- 1 teaspoon Old Bay, or other seafood seasoning

Directions

- Add flour, mayonnaise, dijon, the egg, and the Old Bay to a large bowl. Whisk to combine. Carefully fold in the crab meat, being careful as possible not to separate the lumps of meat. Gently form about 1/2 cup of the crab mixture into a cake about 3 inches wide by 1 inch thick with your palms. Once formed, set aside on a cookie sheet lined with wax paper.

- Heat about 1/2 cup vegetable oil in a heavy-bottomed skillet (I like to use my trusty cast iron pan!) over medium-high heat for 2 minutes. Add crab cakes to hot oil, and fry for about 4 minutes on each side – until nice and golden. Transfer from pan to a paper towel lined plate to drain.
- Serve with cocktail sauce, tartar sauce, and plenty of fresh lemon.

Roast Cod with Garlic Butter

Ingredients
- 1/4 cup unsalted butter, softened
- 1 1/2 tablespoons chopped flat-leaf parsley
- 1 large garlic clove, peeled and minced
- 2 teaspoons minced shallots
- 1/2 teaspoon Dijon mustard
- 1 1/2 tablespoons minced prosciutto di Parma
- 1 tablespoon almond, rice, or all-purpose flour
- 2 tablespoons freshly squeezed lemon juice
- Salt, to taste
- Freshly ground pepper, to taste
- 2 tablespoons canola oil
- 4 (7-ounce) skinless cod fillets
- Garnish: lemon wedges

Directions
- Stir together first 10 ingredients in a small bowl. Set aside.

- Heat oil in a wide, deep, ovenproof skillet over medium-high heat. Season the cod fillets with salt and pepper, and cook 4 minutes. Turn fillets over; cook 1 minute.
- Spoon 1 tablespoon butter mixture over the top of each fillet; transfer skillet to oven, and bake at 450° for 2 minutes or until fish is just cooked through and opaque in the center.
- Add any remaining butter to pan, and let melt, stirring with juices in pan; spoon over fish, and garnish, if desired. Serve immediately.

Balsamic Glazed Salmon

Ingredients
Balsamic Rosemary Glaze
- 1/2 cup balsamic vinegar
- 1/4 cup white wine
- 2 Tbsp honey
- 1 Tbsp dijon mustard
- 1 Tbsp chopped fresh rosemary, divided
- 1 cloves garlic, finely minced
- Salmon
- 4 (6 oz) salmon fillets
- Salt and freshly ground black pepper
- 2 tsp canola oil, divided

Directions

- Allow salmon to rest 10 minutes at room temperature. Meanwhile, in a medium saucepan combine balsamic vinegar, white wine, honey, dijon mustard, 1/2 Tbsp of the chopped rosemary and the garlic.
- Heat mixture over medium-high heat and bring to a boil, then reduce heat and simmer over medium-low heat until sauce has thickened and reduced to 1/3 cup, about 13 - 15 minutes, stirring occasionally. Remove from heat and pour into a heat proof dish (using a rubber spatula to get it all out) and allow to cool.
- Season both sides of salmon with salt and pepper. Heat a large non-stick skillet over medium-high heat and add 1 tsp of canola oil. Once pan and oil are hot, add 2 salmon fillets and cook, without moving, until salmon has nicely browned on bottom, about 3 - 5 minutes.
- Carefully flip salmon to opposite side and continue to cook 3 - 5 minutes longer until bottom is browned and salmon has cooked through. Rest in a warm oven
- Wipe skillet clean, add remaining 1 tsp oil, once hot repeat process with remaining 2 salmon fillets.
- Serve warm drizzling each fillet with balsamic rosemary glaze and sprinkling tops with remaining 1/2 Tbsp of rosemary.

Caribbean Sea Bass

Ingredients
- 1 pound MSC Chilean Sea Bass (or another thick, flaky white fish like cod or halibut – MSC or Green rated preferably)
- 1 tablespoon honey
- olive oil, for the skillet
- ½ a habanero, seeded, diced
- 2 scallions, trimmed, cut into thin rings
- ten 1/4"-thick half-moon slices of pineapple
- 1 avocado, peeled and sliced into 10 wedges
- salt and pepper

Directions
- Cut your fish into two equal portions and season very well with salt. Sprinkle with fresh pepper and drizzle the honey on top, splitting the tablespoon between the two filets.

- Slick the bottom of a 10" or 12" non-stick skillet with olive oil and heat over medium-high heat. When very hot, add the fish, skin-side down. Cook without moving for 3-5 minutes, depending on the thickness. You might want a splatter screen to help keep your stovetop clean.
- When the fish has started to firm up, flip carefully and let the honey caramelize into a nice "crust",

another 3 or 4 minutes. Remove the fish from the skillet and set aside on a warm plate.
- In the skillet place the pineapple moons in a single layer and toss the diced habanero and sliced scallions on top. Season with salt and pepper. After 2 minutes, gently flip the pineapple and cook 2 more minutes. Remove the pineapple, pepper and scallions from the skillet, and set the fish back in to finish cooking. This will not take long.
- To plate: alternate wedges of avocado and pineapple on two plates, sprinkling the scallions and pepper on too. Place one piece of fish on each plate atop the salad. Serve immediately.

Bacon-Wrapped Scallops

Ingredients
- 1 lb Bacon
- 15 Scallops
- 1 tsp Smoked Paprika

Directions
- Preheat oven to 425°F.
- Rinse scallops under cold water.
- Cut bacon strips in half.
- Wrap each scallop with 1/2 strip of bacon.
- Skewer 2–3 bacon-wrapped scallops per skewer.
- Sprinkle with smoked paprika, seasoning both sides.
- Bake at 425°F for 20 minutes.
- Flip, then bake for an additional 15 minutes.

Tuna Patties Recipe

Ingredients

- 2 6-ounce cans tuna
- 2 teaspoons Dijon mustard
- 1/2 cup white bread torn into small pieces
- 1 teaspoon lemon zest
- 1 Tbsp lemon juice
- 1 Tbsp water (or liquid from the cans of tuna)
- 2 Tbsp chopped fresh parsley
- 2 Tbsp chopped fresh chives, green onions, or shallots
- Salt and freshly ground black pepper
- A couple squirts of Crystal hot sauce or tabasco
- 1 raw egg
- 2 Tbsp olive oil
- 1/2 teaspoon butter

Directions

- Drain the liquid from the tuna cans. If you are using tuna packed in water, reserve a tablespoon of the tuna water, and add a teaspoon of olive oil to the tuna mixture in the next step.
- In a medium bowl, mix together the tuna, mustard, torn white bread, lemon zest, lemon juice, water, parsley, chives, and hot sauce. Sprinkle on salt and freshly ground black pepper. Taste the mixture before adding the egg to see if it needs more seasoning to your taste. Mix in the egg.
- Divide the mixture into 4 parts. With each part, form into a ball and then flatten into a patty. Place onto a wax paper lined tray and chill for an hour. (You can skip the chilling if you want, chilling just helps the patties stay together when you cook them.)
- Heat the olive oil and a little butter (for taste) in a cast iron or stick-free skillet on medium high. Gently place the patties in the pan, and cook until nicely browned, 3-4 minutes on each side.
- Serve with wedges of lemon. You can also serve with tartar sauce on slider buns for a tuna burger.

Lemon and Garlic Tilapia (Baked) with Mango Salsa

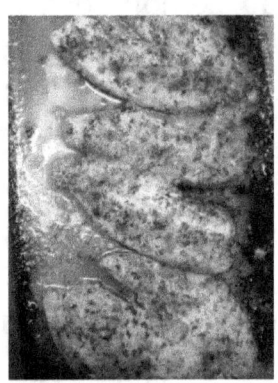

Ingredients
- 3-6 Tilapia filets (6 oz. each)
- 6-8 cloves garlic, crushed and diced large
- 2½ tbsp butter (4 tbsp – if no cooking spray)
- 4 tbsp fresh lemon juice
- 3 tsp fresh Parsley (or dried)
- 1 tsp Oregano (fresh or dried)
- salt and pepper to taste
- cooking spray

Directions
- Preheat oven to 400°.

- Melt 2½ tbsp of butter on a low flame in a small sauce pan. (the rest will be melted and placed into the pan for baking if not cooking spray is available)
- Add garlic and saute on low for about 1 minute. Add all but 1 tbsp of the lemon juice, shut off flame, and remove from heat.

- Spray the bottom of a baking dish lightly with cooking spray (or remaining melted butter) and 1 tbsp of the lemon juice.
- Place the fish on top and season with herbs, salt, and pepper. Pour the lemon butter mixture on the fish and top with fresh parsley for garnish
- Bake at 400° until cooked, about 15 minutes. (or until semi-golden)

Baked fish

Ingredients
- 2-3 whole cleaned fish
- 2 large sliced onions
- 3 large sliced potatoes
- Butter
- 1 lime or lemon

Directions
- The first thing that has to be done is to clean and season the fish. Fish can be bought already cleaned so all you have to do is to season with salt and black pepper.
- Put the fish in a bowl or container of water, pour some fresh lime juice (alternative is white vinegar) into the bowl of fish and leave for about 3-5 minutes. This process is to cut the freshness of the fish.
- Remove the fish from the limed water, wash out the fish with clean water. Season fish with desired seasonings.
- Cut 2-3 sheets of foil that are big enough to contain and wrap each fish.
- Place a tablespoon of butter on one sheet. Use the bottom part of the spoon to spread the butter around the center ofthe sheet of foil.

- Place about two or more slices of potato, side by side, on the sheet of buttered foil, then some sliced onions on top of the potatoes.
- Place one seasoned fish on top of the sliced potatoes and onions. Wrap the foil, containing the fish and other ingredients. Ensure that the sides of the packets are well folded otherwise the sauce from butter will seep out. Repeat the above steps for the rest of the fish.
- After you have finished wrapping all the fish, place them in a baking tray and put the tray in a pre heated oven for approximately 45 minutes.

Stewed Fried Fish

Ingredients
- 4 snapper fillet (you can use any fish you like)
- One sliced tomato
- One sliced onion
- Flour
- Olive oil
- 1 lemon or lime

Directions
- Put the fish in a large bowl of water and squeeze half a lime or lemon into the water. This is to eliminate the fresh scent of the fish. Allow the fish to soak in the lemon/lime water for a few minutes. Then throw out the water. Season the fish with Blended Herbs.
- In a plate, put some flour – about half cup, coat each piece of fish in the flour. Ensure that the pieces of fish are well coated on both sides.
- While that is being done, put a frying pan on the stove to hot. Coat the bottom of the pot with olive oil. When the oil is hot, add the fish.
- Allow the fish to cook – each side of the fish to get golden brown. Remove from the frying pan and put in a plate.
- After all the fish has been fried and removed from the frying pan, add the sliced onion and tomato to

saute. Add half cup of water and allow the vegetables to cook.
- The tomatoes will begin to soften and release its juices – thicken the sauce. You can add two tablespoons of butter at this point. Season with salt and black pepper.
- Add the fried fish to the sauce and let the fish absorb the flavours of the sauce for a few minutes. That is it! Turn off the stove.

Source

Seafood Lasagna

Ingredients

- 1 tablespoon butter
- 1 pound seafood (king crab, shrimp and scallops)
- 1 teaspoon garlic (chopped)
- 1/4 cup white wine (or chicken stock)
- 1 tablespoon lemon juice
- 4 tablespoons butter
- 2 teaspoons garlic (chopped)
- 4 tablespoons flour
- 3 cups milk
- 1/2 cup parmigiano reggiano (grated)
- salt and pepper to taste
- 1/4 cup dill (chopped)
- 1 (16 ounce) container ricotta cheese
- 1 (10 ounce) package spinach (thawed and drained)
- 1 egg
- 1/2 cup parmigiano reggiano (grated)
- 1 cup mozzarella (grated)

- 1/2 pound lasagna noodles (cooked)
- 1/4 cup parmigiano reggiano (grated)
- 1/2 cup mozzarella (grated)

Directions
- Heat the butter in a pan.
- Add the seafood and saute until cooked, just a few minutes and set the seafood aside.
- Add the garlic and saute until fragrant, about a minutes.
- Add the white wine and lemon juice, deglaze the pan, and simmer to reduce by half.
- Add the seafood and toss to coat.
- Melt the butter in a large sauce pan.
- Add the garlic and saute until fragrant, about a minute.
- Add the flour and stir while cooking for a few minutes.
- Slowly whisk in the milk and simmer until it thickens.
- Remove from the heat and mix in the parmigiano reggiano, salt and pepper and dill.
- Mix the ricotta, spinach, egg, parmigiano reggiano, mozzarella and a cup of the white sauce.
- Pour 1/4 cup of the white sauce over the bottom of an 8 inch square baking dish.
- Add a layer of noodles.
- Add a layer of half of the cheese mixture.
- Add a layer of noodles.

- Add a layer of all of the seafood and pour a cup of the white sauce over it.
- Add a layer of noodles.
- Add a layer of the remaining cheese mixture.
- Add a final layer of noodles.
- Pour 1/2 cup of the white sauce over the noodles and top with the parmigiano reggiano and mozzarella.
- Bake in a preheated 350F oven until bubbling on the sides and golden brown on top, about 45-60 minutes.

  Note: This lasagna has 4 layers of noodles so make sure that you cook the right amount.

Grilled Seafood Packs with Lemon-Chive Butter

Ingredients

Seafood Packets
- 32 shell clams (littlenecks or cherrystones)
- 32 uncooked medium shrimp in shells (about 1 1/4 lb), thawed if frozen
- 32 sea scallops (about 2 1/2 lb)
- 4 ears fresh sweet corn, husks removed, cleaned, cut into fourths
- 32 large cherry tomatoes

Lemon-Chive Butter
- 1/3 cup butter or margarine, melted
- 2 teaspoons grated lemon peel
- 2 teaspoons chopped fresh or 1/2 teaspoon freeze-dried chives
- Fresh chive stems or chopped fresh **chives**, if desired

Directions

- Heat gas or charcoal grill. Cut 8 (18x12-inch) sheets of heavy-duty foil; spray with cooking spray.
- Place 4 clams, shrimp and scallops in center of each sheet; top each with 2 pieces of corn and 4 tomatoes. In small bowl, mix butter ingredients. Drizzle about 2 teaspoons butter over seafood and vegetables in each packet.
- Bring up 2 sides of foil so edges meet. Seal edges, making tight 1/2-inch fold; fold again, allowing space for heat circulation and expansion. Fold other sides to seal.
- Place packets on grill over medium heat. Cover grill; cook 15 to 20 minutes, rotating packets 1/2 turn after 10 minutes, or until clam shells have opened, shrimp are pink, and scallops are white and opaque. (Cooking time may vary depending on ingredients selected) Discard any clams that don't open.
- To serve, cut large X across top of each packet; carefully fold back foil to allow steam to escape. Top with chives.

Conch Fritters

Ingredients
- Conch
- 2 tablespoon flour
- 3 finely grated garlic cloves
- 1 diced onion
- Salt
- Olive oil
- Pepper sauce (optional)
- Chive

Directions
- Cleaning the conch: Simply place the conch in a pot of water and allow it to boil for an hour. After the time is up, remove the conch from the pot of water and use a knife the scrap/peel off the skin.
- Now even though the conch was boiling for an hour, it was still a bit chewy so you may have to pressurize it a bit. So put the conch in a pressure pot and allow it to pressurize for about 25 minutes.
- Cut up the conch as small as possible, add the onion, garlic. Cut about 2 inches of the green part of the chive and thinly slice. Add to the conch mixture. Add the flour, be careful not to add too

much flour otherwise the flavor of the conch will be lost.
- Mix everything together and gradually add some water until the mixture is glue like. Don't let the mixture get too watery.
- Put a frying pan on the stove to hot and add some olive oil. Add a tablespoon of the conch fritter mixture to the pot. Repeat this step until all the mixture is used up. As the bottom of each fritter begin to get brown, turn them over and allow the other side to cook and get golden brown.
- Remove from frying pan and serve.

Source

Bubba's Crab Stew

Ingredients
- 1/2 cup fennel bulb, trimmed and chopped
- 1 stalk celery, chopped
- 1/4 cup yellow onion, chopped
- 1 stick butter
- 3/4 cup self-rising flour
- 2 tablespoons crab base, (or seafood bouillon)
- 2 quarts heavy cream
- 2 tablespoons cooking sherry
- 2 cups half and half

- 1 quart milk
- 2 lbs crabmeat, picked clean of shells
- salt, to taste
- pepper, to taste

Preparation

- In a food processor, finely chop the fennel, celery and onion. Melt the butter on medium-high heat in a large heavy saucepan. Add the vegetables and sauté until soft. Stir in the flour until it is all absorbed and no lumps remain. Continue to stir and cook the mixture for 8 to 10 minutes, until it spreads out and becomes bubbly.
- Stir in the crab base, heavy cream, sherry, half and half and milk. Bring the mixture to a boil, then reduce the heat to a low simmer. Allow the stew to thicken for no more than 8 to 10 minutes, then remove from heat

Lobster Mac and Cheese

Ingredients
- 1 pound elbow pasta (or any short cut pasta)
- 9 tablespoons butter
- 1 clove garlic
- 1 pound cooked lobster meat, chopped
- 1 tablespoon fresh parsley, plus more for garnish
- 1 1/2 cups crushed Ritz crackers (about 1 sleeve)

- 1/4 cup flour
- 3 cups whole milk
- 1 1/4 cups sharp white cheddar cheese, shredded
- 1 1/4 cups gruyere cheese, shredded
- 1 cup fontina cheese, shredded
- 4 ounces brie, rind removed and chopped
- 1/4 teaspoon mustard powder
- 1/4 teaspoon cayenne
- 1/4 teaspoon salt
- 1/2 teaspoon pepper

Directions

- Preheat oven to 350 degrees F. Spray a baking dish with nonstick spray.
- Bring a large pot of salted water to a boil. Boil the pasta until al-dente. You want it to have a bit of bite because it will finish cooking in the oven. Drain well.
- While the pasta boils add 3 tablespoons butter to a medium skillet and melt. Add the garlic and sauté 30 seconds then add in the lobster meat and sauté for 3-5 minutes. Add the parsley and cook another 30 seconds. Remove the lobster from the pan.
- Add another 2 tablespoon of butter to the skillet. Throw in the crushed Ritz crackers and toss to coat. Toast the crumbs for 3-5 minutes, stirring frequently to avoid burning. Once the crumbs are lightly toasted, remove from the heat and set aside.
- In the same pot you boiled the pasta, melt the remaining 4 tablespoons butter over medium heat.

Whisk in the flour. Reduce the heat to medium-low and let cook and bubble for 1 minute, stirring once or twice to avoid burning. Gradually whisk in the milk and raise the heat up to medium-high. Bring the mixture to a boil, whisking frequently until the sauce has thickened, about 2-3 minutes. Remove from the heat and stir in all of the cheese, mustard powder, cayenne, salt and pepper. Stir until the cheese is fully melted. Stir in the pasta and about 3/4 of the lobster meat. Transfer to the prepared baking dish.
- Evenly sprinkle on the remaining lobster chunks and then the toasted cracker crumbs. Place the baking dish on a baking sheet.
- Bake for 20 minutes or until the crumbs are golden brown and the sauce is bubbling.
    - Remove from the oven and let sit five minutes

Perfectly Seared Scallops

Ingredients
- 1 pound sea scallops, patted dry
- 1 tablespoon unsalted butter
- 1 tablespoon olive oil
- Freshly ground sea salt
- Freshly ground black pepper
- Lemon for squeezing, optional

Directions
- Remove tiny side muscle from the scallops if they have them, then rinse with cold water and pat dry with a paper towel.
- Add the butter and oil to a large saute pan over high heat.

- Generously salt and pepper the scallops. Once the butter/oil combo begins to smoke, gently add the scallops, making sure they are not touching.
- Sear scallops for 1 1/2 minutes on each side - not touching them at all while they're searing. The scallops should have a nice golden crust on each side and be translucent in the center. Serve right away!!!

Shrimp Fried Rice

Ingredients

- 3 tablespoons soy sauce
- 1 tablespoons sesame oil
- 1/2 teaspoon ginger powder
- 1/2 teaspoon white pepper
- 2 tablespoons olive oil
- 1 pound medium shrimp, peeled and deveined
- Kosher salt and freshly ground black pepper, to taste
- 2 cloves garlic, minced
- 1 onion, diced
- 2 carrots, peeled and grated
- 1/2 cup frozen corn
- 1/2 cup frozen peas
- 3 cups cooked rice

- 2 green onions, sliced

Directions

- In a small bowl, whisk together soy sauce, sesame oil, ginger powder and white pepper; set aside.
- Heat olive oil in a large skillet or wok over medium high heat. Add shrimp, and cook, stirring occasionally, until pink, about 2-3 minutes; season with salt and pepper, to taste; set aside.
- Add garlic and onion to the skillet, and cook, stirring often, until onions have become translucent, about 3-4 minutes. Stir in carrots, corn and peas, and cook, stirring constantly, until vegetables are tender, about 3-4 minutes.
- Stir in rice, green onions and soy sauce mixture. Cook, stirring constantly, until heated through, about 2 minutes. Stir in shrimp.
- Serve immediately.

Calamari Fritti with Pepperoncini Aioli

Ingredients

- 1 pound squid bodies, rinsed, patted dry with paper towels and sliced into 1/2-inch rings
- 1 cup milk
- 1 extra large egg
- 2 cups unbleached all-purpose flour
- 1/4 teaspoon dried basil
- 1 teaspoon paprika
- Kosher salt and freshly ground black pepper
- Vegetable oil for frying

Accompaniments

- Lemon wedges
- Pepperoncini Aioli, recipe follows

Directions

- In a medium bowl, whisk together the milk and egg. Add the squid rings, cover with plastic wrap, and refrigerate for at least 20 minutes and up to an hour.
- Pour about 2 inches of oil in a fryer or large, heavy pot and heat the oil to 375º F. In a pie plate, whisk together the flour, basil, paprika, then season the mixture with salt and freshly ground black pepper.
- Toss a few of the calamari at a time in the seasoned flour to coat. Fry for 2-3 minutes or until golden brown.
- Using a slotted spoon, transfer the fried calamari to paper towels to drain. Season with a sprinkle of kosher salt.
- Serve immediately with lemon wedges and Pepperoncini Aioli. Enjoy!

Pepperoncini Aioli
- 8-10 pepperoncini peppers, stems removed, drained and roughly chopped
- 1 medium garlic clove, minced
- 2 Tablespoons chopped fresh flat-leaf parsley
- 1/2 cup mayonnaise
- 1 Tablespoon pepperoncini pickle juice
- Kosher salt and freshly ground black pepper

Directions
- In the bowl of food processor, process the peppers, garlic, and parsley until finely chopped. (You may

need to scrape down the sides of the bowl a few times).
- Add the mayonnaise and pickle juice and process until combined. Season to taste with salt and pepper.
- Transfer to a serving bowl and refrigerate until ready to use. Enjoy!

Stuffed Mushrooms

Ingredients
- 24 ounces, White Button Mushrooms
- 1/3 pound Hot Pork Sausage
- ½ whole Medium Onion, Finely Diced
- 4 cloves Garlic, Finely Minced
- 8 ounces, Cream Cheese

- 1 whole Egg Yolk
- ¾ cups Parmesan Cheese, Grated
- 1/3 cup Dry White Wine
- Salt And Pepper

Directions

- Wipe off or wash mushrooms in cold water. Pop out stems, reserving both parts.
- Chop mushroom stems finely and set aside.
- Brown and crumble sausage. Set aside on a plate to cool.
- Add onions and garlic to the same skillet; cook for 2 minutes over medium low heat. Pour in wine to deglaze pan, allow liquid to evaporate. Add in chopped mushroom stems, stir to cook for 2 minutes. Add salt and pepper to taste. Set mixture aside on a plate to cool.
- In a bowl, combine cream cheese and egg yolk. Stir together with Parmesan cheese. Add cooled sausage and cooled mushroom stems. Stir mixture together and refrigerate for a short time to firm up.
- Smear mixture into the cavity of each mushroom, creating a sizable mound over the top.
- Bake at 350 degrees for 20 to 25 minutes, or until golden brown. Allow to cool at least ten minutes before serving; the stuffed mushrooms taste better when not piping hot. Garnish with minced parsley if you're feeling fancy.

Grace Shrimp Curry

Ingredients
- 2 tablespoons margarine
- 1/4 cup finely chopped onion
- 2 cloves garlic, finely chopped
- 1 1/2 tablespoons all purpose flour
- 1 Tbsp. curry powder
- 1 Tbsp. lime juice
- 1 1/2 cups lemon juice
- 1 1/2 cups *stock
- 1/4 tsp. salt
- 1 tsp. GRACE HOT PEPPER SAUCE
- 1 Tbsp. chopped parsley

Directions
- Melt margarine in a heated frying pan, fry onions and garlic lightly.
- Add flour, curry powder and cook for 3-4 minutes, stirring constantly to avoid burning.
- Add lemon juice, stock, salt and Grace Hot Pepper Sauce.
  Stir and allow to cook over low heat for about 3-4 minutes.
- Add more stock if necessary and season to taste. Stir in the shrimp and allow to heat thoroughly. Garnish with parsley.

Barbecued Fish Rolls

Ingredients
- 500 gram fish fillets
- 1/4 tsp. salt & Grace Black Pepper
- 1/2 cup sweet pepper
- 2 Tbs. clove garlic
- ½ cup plum tomatoes
- 2 Tbs. onions
- 1 cup Grace Jerk Barbecue Sauce

Directions
- Preheat oven at 185°C.
- Season fillets with salt and pepper, roll and place in a baking dish. Chop sweet pepper, garlic and tomatoes.
- Mince onion and place in a bowl, pour in Grace Jerk Barbeque Sauce and stir.
- Pour mixture over fish. Bake in preheated oven.

Baked Fish with Yam Stuffing

Ingredients
- 1 kg. whole fish
- 1 tsp. salt
- 1 tsp. white pepper
- 1 tsp. garlic powder
- 500 grams yam

Directions
- Preheat oven to 180 degrees C/350 degrees F. Season fish using salt, white pepper and garlic powder.
- Dice and cook yam for stuffing.
- Stuff yam into cavity of fish. Seal the opening by using a sterilized needle and thread or by using a skewer.
- Place on a lightly greased tray and put to bake. Baste at regular intervals (to retain moisture and improve flavour) until done.

Brown Fish Stew

Ingredients
- 2lb. Fish (any type filleted or not)
- 1 Medium Onion (chopped)
- 1 Green Bell Pepper(chopped)
- 1 tblsp. Salt
- 1 tblsp. Black-pepper
- 1 sprg. Thyme
- 1/4 oz. Mushroom Soy Sauce
- 1/4 oz. Grace Browning
- 2 cl. Garlic
- 1 oz Lime Juice
- 1 Scotch Bonnet Pepper
- 10 oz. Water
- 1/4 oz. Ginger Root

Directions
- Wash the fish in a lime juice/water solution. Dry the fish with a paper hand towel or cloth to remove all the juice and water; this will stop any potential hot splashes from the hot oil in the skillet, when the fish in placed into the hot oil later on.
- Rub a pinch of salt and pepper on each piece of fish. Heat the oil in the skillet on high for 2 minutes or so, then turn the heat to medium. Carefully place fish into the oil in the skillet.
- Pan-fry fish until golden brown. During the frying process, do not move the fish around in the skillet

- because this will cause the pieces of fish to break into small pieces.
- Its Jamaican Brown Stew Fish you're making, not fish salad.
- Remove fish from skillet.
- Discard the oil and replace with fresh oil. Sauté the onions, garlic and green bell peppers together. Cover the pot for 1 minute, while the vegetables sizzle.
- Next add water to the vegetables and allow the vegetables to cook for another five minutes.
- Now add the ginger root, mushroom soy sauce, scotch bonnet pepper, thyme and browning.
- Cover the pot and cook for 5 minutes, add salt to taste and then add fish to stew and simmer for 3 minutes.
- Serve with dumplings, or rice & peas, or white rice, or pasta, yam & banana, or bread.

Here is a sauce you may like to put on your Brown Stew Fish.

Ingredients
- 8 Scotch Bonnet Peppers (chopped)
- 2 slices Cho Cho (Christophine)
- 1 Carrot
- 1 small Onion (chopped)
- Vinegar
- 12 Pimento Seeds (Allspice)
- 1 16oz. Glass Jar or Bottle

Directions

- Cut the carrot long ways into 4 pieces. You can further pattern the pieces if you like. Do the same for the cho cho.
- Place the pieces of carrot and cho cho inside the bottle vertically. Alternate the pieces so you will get an orange and green pattern.
- Now add a ¼ of the amount of the scotch bonnet peppers with four pimento seed, and onions to the jar. If you can, press the peppers into the jar with a small spoon.
- Repeat this process until you get everything into the jar. Pour the vinegar onto the ingredients, and then tighten the jar's cover. Let this sit for 1 week or longer before using.

Zuppa di Pesce (seafood soup)

Ingredients
- 6 Sea Scallops
- 8 Small Shrimps
- 1/2 lobster tail
- 1 ounce of oregano
- 1/2 ounce of basil
- 4 ounce of snapper
- 1 large shrimp (jumbo)
- 2 ounce of plum tomato (diced)
- 1/2 ounce of parsley and a
- Pinch of red pepper

Directions
- Pour 1 ounce of the oil into a hot pan with the lobster tail and fish sauté for about 2 minutes then add the plum tomato and fresh herbs.
- Add 1/4 pint of fish stock and lease to cook for at least 5 minutes.

Crespoline Cosimo

Ingredients
- 1 Crepe
- 2 oz. of basil
- 1/2 chopped onion
- 2 fl. oz. of cream
- 2 oz chopped shrimp
- 3 fl. oz. of béchamel
- 6 fl. oz. of white wine
- 1 oz. chopped basil leaf
- 4 fl. oz. of heavy cream
- 1 oz. diced lobster tail
- 1 oz. diced small shrimps
- 2 oz. of fine breadcrumbs
- 1 chopped clove garlic clove

Directions
- First you need to use the olive oil to lightly sauté the onions including the garlic. Now cook the lobster and shrimp slowly.
- Add cream and the basil. Reduce the heat for two minutes. Next add the remaining ingredients and let the mixture cool off before filling the crepe.

Preparations for sauce
- Now use the butter to sauté the shallots then add the white wine. Reduce the heat.

- Add the dropped shrimps along with basil, cook for 1 more minute.
- Finish by adding the cream, béchamel seasoning for flavor.

Conch Pie or Conch Stew

Ingredients
- 3 onions
- 2 green peppers
- 2 teaspoons thyme
- 5 pounds of conch
- 2 teaspoons black pepper
- 2 tablespoons pick-a-pepper
- milk, with 4 cans of water
- 1 tablespoon of salt to taste
- 2 to 3 coconuts to 5 to 6 cups of water or 2 cans
- 1 green or red bell pepper (chopped)
- 3 strips of crispy dried bacon crushed
- 3 tablespoons margarine or oil to fry onion & coconut.

Directions
- First pound very well the conch. Place the slices in a pot then cover with the coconut water adding more water if needed to cover, and scald, bringing to a boil and simmer for about 20 minutes until its tender.
- Mix together with the other ingredients and cook for about 40 minutes. Finally, add the pie on top simmer until cooked.
- "Pie" or home-made noodles about 2 Cups of the flour, water and salt for pie.

Preparations For Pie:

- Use a little bit of the water and salt to mix with the flour until you have a nice workable dough, kneading the dough a few times.
- Next Pull Off! 1 piece about the size of your whole thumb. Flatten out by placing the dough between two thumbs and fore finger to flatten, then lay on top of the slightly bubbling stew.

Salmon Filet with Mango Cilantro Salsa

Ingredients
- 4 6-ounce portions salmon filet
- Mango Cilantro Salsa
- 1 ripe mango, peeled and 1/2-inch diced
- 1/4 cup chopped scallion, green part only
- 1/4 cup diced red bell pepper
- 1 tablespoon finely diced fresh jalapeno
- 1 tablespoon chopped fresh cilantro
- 1 small clove garlic, minced
- 1 tablespoon freshly squeezed lime juice
- 1/4 teaspoon salt
- 1/2 teaspoon extra-virgin olive oil

Directions
- Bake salmon filet at 400F for 15 to 20 minutes, depending on the thickness of the salmon.
- For Mango Cilantro Salsa, lightly toss all ingredients in bowl.
- Chill in refrigerator for at least 1 hour for flavors to meld.

Grilled Maple Mustard Salmon

Ingredients
- 2/3 cup melted butter
- 1/2 tablespoon dried dill
- 1/2 cup maple syrup
- 1/4 cup Dijon style mustard
- 4 salmon filets, with skin
- vegetable oil

Directions
- In a small saucepan, blend first four ingredients over low heat until melted together.
- Place salmon in a glass dish and pour marinade over salmon. Refrigerate for about an hour. Preheat grill or broiler to high.
- Remove salmon from marinade; reserve marinade. Brush skin side generously with oil and place on grill or on the rack of a roasting pan.
- Grill or broil salmon, basting frequently with reserved marinade. Remove from heat when just cooked through.

Cape Mudge Halibut Chowder

Ingredients
- 2 Tablespoons Olive Oil
- 5 Medium Carrots — Chopped
- 3 Stalks Celery — Chopped
- 2 Large Onion — Chopped
- 4 Cloves Garlic — Chopped
- 5 Cups Chicken Stock
- 2 Cans Tomatoes — Chopped
- 1 Teaspoon Oregano
- 1/2 Teaspoon Salt
- 1/2 Teaspoon Pepper
- 1 Medium Bay Leaf
- 1 Medium Red Bell Pepper — Chopped
- 1 Medium Green Bell Pepper — Chopped
- 2 Pounds Halibut — Cubed

Directions
- Sauté carrots, celery, onion and garlic in oil for 10 minutes.
- Add stock, tomatoes, oregano, salt, pepper and bay leaf.
- Bring a boil and simmer for 30 minutes. Add red and green peppers.
- Simmer for 15 minutes. Add fish and simmer for 7 minutes. Remove bay leaf and serve.

Baked Halibut With Tarragon Crust

Ingredients

- 1 Cup Sour Cream
- 3 Tablespoons Tarragon — Chopped
- 1 Bunch Scallion — Chopped
- 1 Clove Garlic — Chopped
- 1 Dash Hot Sauce
- 1 Dash Worcestershire Sauce
- Pepper — To Taste
- 1 Cup Bread Crumbs
- 1/2 Cup Parmesan Cheese
- 1/2 Cup Swiss Cheese — Shredded
- 1/4 Cup Parsley — Chopped
- 2 Pounds Halibut Steak

Directions

- Combine sour cream, tarragon, green onion, garlic, hot sauce, Worcestershire sauce and pepper. In another bowl, combine bread crumbs, both cheeses, and parsley.
- Dip fish in sour cream mixture then roll in bread crumb mixture. Place on baking sheet and bake for 12 minute in 500 degree oven. Serve.

Steamed Fish

Ingredients

- 1 whole fish (3 lbs), cleaned, with the head left on
- 1½ tsp (7 ml) salt
- 2 inch (5 cm) piece of fresh ginger root
- 4 scallions
- 1 tablespoon (15 ml) soy sauce
- 1 teaspoon (5 ml) sesame seed oil
- 3 tablespoons (45 ml) rice wine or dry sherry

Directions

- Cut deep gashes into the sides of the fish, about ¾ inch (2 cm) apart; it does not matter if the gashes hit the bone.
- Rub the salt all over the fish, inside the cavity as well as on the skin outside, then put the fish on a plate or in a shallow bowl.
- Slice the ginger thinly. Clean the scallions, then cut into 1 inch (2 ½ cm) lengths.
- Put half the scallions and ginger into the cavity of the fish. Carefully sprinkle the soy sauce and sesame oil over the fish, then spread the rest of the ginger and scallions on top. Pour one or two inches (2 ½ or 5 cm) of water into a wok. Put the plate in a steamer tray and set the tray over the water.
- Sprinkle the wine or sherry over the fish.

- Bring the water to a boil, then cover the steamer and steam the fish for 20 to 25 minutes.
- Remove from the steamer carefully and serve the fish immediately.

Sea Trout Salad

Ingredients
- 1 lb middle cut sea trout
- 1 lb yams
- 2 large firm tomatoes
- ½ medium-sized cucumbers
- 1 head lettuce
- Salt and pepper to taste
- ½ lb cabbage
- 1 tbsp finely chopped herbs
- 1 large lime
- 6 tbsp mayonnaise

Directions
- Clean and season the fish with salt, pepper and lime juice and leave in the refrigerator overnight, or at least 3 – 4 hours before cooking.
- Scrub, peel and boil the yams, then cut into neat cubes.
  Steam the fish, remove the skin and bones and flake using a fork.
- Add cubed yams to the flaked fish, add chopped herbs and blend carefully with 3 tablespoons of mayonnaise, again using the fork. Do not crush.
- Finely shred the cabbage, cut the cucumber into neat cubes and tomatoes into neat chunks. Toss

altogether with the remaining 3 tablespoons of mayonnaise.
- Wash the lettuce leaves and keep whole.
- Arrange the lettuce leaves on a dish, pile the prepared fish mixture in the centre, and arrange the "tossed" vegetables around the fish.

Scrambled Fish

Ingredients
- 2 cups flaked fish
- 4 eggs
- 4 slices hot buttered toast
- 2 tbsp. milk
- 4 tbsp. butter or fat
- A little mustard
- Salt and pepper to taste

Directions
- Beat the eggs slightly just enough to mix yolks and whites. Season with salt, pepper and mustard if liked.
- Add the milk and then the flaked fish.
- Melt the butter in a strong saucepan, and meanwhile make the toast.
- Put the fish mixture into the hot butter and stir gently until mixture thickens.
- Butter the toast and pile the scrambled fish on top.

Baked Crab Guadeloupe-Style

Ingredients
- 454 g (1 lb.) crab meat
- 125 ml (1/2 cup) green bell pepper, seeded and finely chopped
- 1 clove of garlic, minced
- 60 ml (1/4 cup) dry sherry
- 60 ml (1/4 cup) chopped parsley
- 1/4 tsp. red chili powder
- A pinch of mace
- Salt and pepper
- 1 egg
- Juice of 1 lime
- 2 + 4 tbsp. butter
- 250 ml (1 cup) fresh bread crumbs + 2 tbsp.

Directions
- Butter a baking sheet with 1 tbsp. butter; in a bowl, crumble the crabmeat and blend in the bread crumbs;
- melt 1 tbsp. butter in a skillet; add the bell pepper and garlic; cook for 5 minutes over medium heat until tender but not browned;
- remove the skillet from the heat; add the sherry and lime juice; mix in the parsley, chili powder, mace, salt and pepper;

- mix everything into the crab-bread crumb mixture and combine well;
- pour the mixture onto the baking sheet; spread out gently with a spatula;
- sprinkle with 2 tbsp. bread crumbs and dot with 4 tbsp. butter;
- bake in a preheated 180° C (350° F) oven for 30 minutes or until browned; serve immediately.

Caribbean-Style Crabs

Ingredients
- 8 tbs. Butter
- 4 Scallions chopped
- 1-2 tsp. chopped garlic
- 1 hot green chili – finely chopped and seeded
- 1 tbs. Curry powder
- ¾-1 LB crab meat – shredded
- 2 tbs. Chopped fresh coriander leaves
- 2 tbs. Finely chopped parsley
- Salt & freshly ground pepper
- 6-8 tbs. crab liquid or clam broth
- 2 cups Bread crumbs

Directions
- Melt butter in skillet; add scallions, garlic and chili peppers and cook until scallions are wilted.
- Add curry powder to this mixture and blend thoroughly. Add crab, coriander and parsley.
- Add salt, pepper and crab liquid (if more is needed, add melted butter).
- Blend in bread crumbs. Fill the mixture in 8 clam shells and bake at 400°F about 10 minutes or until browned.

Fish Loaf

Ingredients
- 1 lb minced fish
- 1 cup soft bread crumbs
- 1 egg (beaten)
- 1 tsp lime juice
- 1 tsp black pepper
- 3 tbsps chopped herbs
- ½ tsp ground clove

Directions
- Combine all ingredients and mix well. Put into greased loaf tin and bake in a moderate oven (350°) for 20-30 minutes. Slice on the diagonal. Serve with a green salad.

Thai-Dyed Seafood Soup

Ingredients
- 6 Cups Water
- 6 Kaffir Lime Leaves — halved Or
- 2 Peels Lime — chopped
- 2 Inch Ginger Root — chopped
- 1 Bunch Scallions — chopped
- 1 Medium Lemon — thinly sliced
- 2 Medium Jalapeno — chopped
- Salt And Pepper — to taste
- 1/2 Pound Salmon — cubed
- 1/4 Cup Fresh Basil — stripped
- Palm Vinegar — or white vinegar
- Red Chile Paste — to taste

Directions
- Bring water, lime leaves, ginger root, scallions, lemon and jalapenos to a boil. Reduce heat, simmer for 8 minutes. Add salt, pepper and salmon.
- Simmer until the salmon changes color. Place into bowl, garnish with basil, vinegar and chili paste.

Lobster Eggs Benedict With Crispy Potato Pancakes & Bearnaise Sauce

Ingredients
- the meat of 1 cooked/steamed lobster

For the Crispy Potato Pancakes
- 4 medium potatoes (Russet or Yukon Gold)
- 1/2 cup diced onions
- salt and pepper
- 1 Tbsp. corn starch
- oil for frying

For the Home Fry Croutons:
- 2-3 slices of cubed country bread (crusts removed)
- olive oil for frying
- 1 clove of minced garlic
- salt and pepper
- fresh thyme leaves
- Poached eggs
- 4 large eggs
- Water
- white vinegar

Béarnaise Sauce:
- 1/2 cup melted butter
- 3 eggs yolks
- 1 Tbsp. white wine
- 1 Tbsp. lemon juice
- pinch of salt

- dash of Tabasco Sauce
- 1 tsp. chopped fresh tarragon

Garnish:
- chopped fresh chives
- sweet paprika or lobster roe
- fresh ground pepper

Directions

- Boil your lobster for about 10 minutes then drain and place in an ice water bath to halt the cooking. Remove the meat from the shells, reserve.
- Peel your potatoes and with the side of the box grater with the largest hole, grate the potatoes into a sieve. Sprinkle some course salt and toss then allow to steep for 15 minutes.
- Drizzle some olive oil into a skillet over medium heat and add the cubed bread and garlic and stir until browned and crispy. Remove with a slotted spoon and reserve.
- Use your hands to squeeze excess water from the potatoes and add into a bowl along with the diced onions, salt, pepper and corn starch and toss.
- Pour about 1/2 inch of oil in a heavy-bottomed skillet over medium-high heat and place a handful of grated potato in the pan and press down with a spatula to flatten.
- Fill the skillet for 2-3 more potato pancakes and fry for about 3-4 minutes a side (flip the pancakes when golden-brown).

- Blot excess oil with paper towel and place your potato pancakes on your serving plates along with the reserved Home Fry Croutons in a warm oven (250F). Place your lobster on the stove to warm up using the residual heat of the oven.
- Add about two inches of water into a large skillet and bring up to a boil over medium-high heat. Crack your eggs and place each one in a ramekin. Add a few drops of vinegar and swirl the hot water with a spoon. Now gently drop each egg into the water, turn off the heat and cover. Allow the eggs to poach for 3-5 minutes (as soon as the whites have cooked you're safe to remove the eggs).
- Prepare your Béarnaise by adding the yolks, lemon juice, wine, Tabasco into a blender/food processor and whiz until well amalgamated. Heat your butter on your stovetop over medium heat.
- Carefully remove with a slotted spoon and ensure excess water has drained from the eggs.
- Cut up your lobster meat, remove the potato pancakes from the oven and place on top of your potato pancakes and then carefully place a poached egg on top of the lobster.
- Time to finish the Béarnaise, slowly pour hot butter into your running blender/food processor until the sauce has thickened and turned to a soft yellow colour. Add a pinch of salt, adjust seasoning and spoon over the eggs.
- Garnish with chopped fresh chives, sweet paprika or lobster roe and fresh ground pepper.

Tamarind Shrimp

Ingredients
- 3 Pounds Medium Shrimp
- 1/4 Cup Tamarind Paste — dissolved in
- 1/2 Cup Water
- 1 Tablespoon Sugar
- 1 Teaspoon Salt
- 1 Teaspoon Pepper
- 1/3 Cup Olive Oil

Directions
- Marinate shrimp in remaining ingredients except oil for 30 minutes.
- Drain and discard marinade. Heat oil in skillet and fry shrimp for 2 minutes.
- Serve with rice.

Sour And Hot Fish

Ingredients
- 3 Tablespoons Olive Oil
- 1 Teaspoon Lemon Grass
- 1 Inch Ginger — finely chopped
- 2 Cloves Garlic — finely chopped
- 2 Medium Dried Chiles — crumbled
- 1 Large Onion — sliced
- 2 Medium Shallot — sliced
- 2 Pounds Red Snapper
- 1 Tablespoon White Vinegar
- 1 Tablespoon Soy Sauce
- 1 Teaspoon Sugar
- 1 Tablespoon Tomato Paste
- 1 Tablespoon Ketchup
- 1/2 Cup Water

Directions
- Directions Heat oil in skillet, add lemongrass, ginger, garlic, chilies, onion and shallots.
- Fry for 3 minutes. Add fish and fry for 2 minutes on each side. Set aside.
- Mix remaining ingredients, pour over the fish and simmer over low for 5 minutes. Serve with rice.

Chile Prawns

Ingredients
- 2 Tablespoons Peanut Oil
- 1 Tablespoon Garlic — chopped
- 1 Tablespoon Ginger — finely chopped
- 2 Large Jalapeno — finely chopped
- 1 Pound Prawns — shelled
- 1 Tablespoon Black Miso
- 1 Medium Tomato — chopped
- 3 Medium Scallion — finely chopped
- 1 Cup Bamboo Shoots
- 1 Tablespoon Soy Sauce
- 2 Tablespoons Rice Wine
- 1 Teaspoon Sugar
- 1/2 Teaspoon Sesame Oil
- 1 Tablespoon Cornstarch
- 1 Tablespoon Water
- Cilantro — for garnish
- Rice

Directions
- Stir-fry in oil, garlic, ginger, and jalapeno. Stir-fry 1 minute. Add the prawns and stir-fry 2 minutes.
- Add mso, tomato, scallion, bamboo shoots, soy sauce, sherry, sugar, and sesame oil.
- Stir-fry 3 minutes. Add cornstarch to water and add to wok.

- Simmer for 1 minute to thicken.
- Garnish with cilantro and serve over rice.

Costa Rican Tilapia

Ingredients
- 3 tablespoons fresh lime juice
- 3 tablespoons olive oil, divided
- 4 tablespoons finely chopped fresh cilantro or parsley, divided
- 4 teaspoons minced garlic, divided
- 1-1/2 teaspoons kosher salt, divided
- 1/4 teaspoon sugar
- 6 tilapia fillets, about 5 ounces each
- 3/4 cup long-grain rice
- 1 cup chopped onions
- 2 oranges, peeled, seeded, coarsely chopped
- 1 can (28 ounces) diced tomatoes, undrained
- 1 can (15 ounces) black or pinto beans, drained, rinsed
- 1 teaspoon dried oregano leaves
- 1/2 teaspoon freshly ground black pepper
- 1/4 teaspoon cayenne pepper

Directions
- For the tilapia marinade, combine lime juice, 1 tablespoon olive oil, 2 tablespoons cilantro, 1 teaspoon garlic, 1/2 teaspoon salt, and sugar in a shallow dish. Add tilapia and marinate 15 minutes, turning once.

- To prepare the bean and rice mixture, cook the rice according to package directions and keep warm while the tilapia is marinating. Preheat oven to 400 degrees. In a large, high-sided skillet or saucepan, heat 2 tablespoons olive oil on medium heat.
- Add remaining garlic and onions; sauté until translucent, about 5 minutes, stirring. Add 2 tablespoons cilantro, oranges, tomatoes, beans, oregano, 1 teaspoon salt, pepper, and cayenne. Cook, uncovered, until hot, 7 to 8 minutes, stirring occasionally.
- Transfer hot rice to a 9 by 13 inch or 2-1/2 to 3 quart baking dish. Spoon the bean mixture on top of rice and gently blend. Slightly overlap tilapia fillets on top and scrape marinade over fillets. Bake until the flesh of the tilapia just begins to flake at the nudge of a fork, 16 to 20 minutes.

Roatan Honduras Conch Soup

Ingredients
- CONCH 4 medium, pounded and chopped
- 2 ONIONS, chopped
- 1/2 cup VEGETABLE OIL
- SALT and PEPPER to taste
- JUICE OF 3 LEMONS
- 2 cans (28 oz. ea.) TOMATOES, chopped
- 1 1/2 cup POTATOES, peeled and chunked
- 4 stalks CELERY, cut into bite-size pieces
- 4 CARROTS, cut into bite-size pieces
- 2 cups WATER
- 1/4 tsp. HOT PEPPER SAUCE
- 2 cups sliced OKRA
- 2 BAY LEAVES
- 1/2 tsp. PARSLEY

Directions
- In a large kettle, sauté onions in oil until translucent. Add salt and pepper.
- Add lemon juice, tomatoes and conch and increase heat.
- Add vegetables and rest of ingredients. Bring to a boil, then simmer for 3 hours. Remove bay leaves and serve.

Almond Tree Snapper with Lemon Herbed Butter

Ingredients
- 2 eggs beaten
- 3 tablespoons of butter
- 8 ounces of filet (snapper)
- 1 cup of all-purpose Flour
- 2 cups of fine breaded crumbs
- 1 cup of almonds lightly salted
- Pinch of black pepper
- Pinch of salt

Directions
- First rinse the fish filet and pat dry, next season Snapper on both sides with black pepper and salt to taste. In a food processor, run the machine in short bursts and grind the bread crumbs and almonds to a fine powder.
- In a shallow bowl add the mixture. Place the flour in another bowl and the eggs in a third bowl. Before serving, melt the butter right in a large frying pan, over medium heat.
- Next dip each side of the fish into the flour first shaking off excess, then in the mixture, then the almond bread crumbs then pan fry fish until golden brown and crusty.

- Fry the fish for about 2 minutes per side, drain and transfer to a plate and sprinkle with the lemon herb butter.

Beer Batter Fish

Ingredients
- 1 cup of flour (extra flour)
- 1/4 teaspoon of pepper
- 2 pounds of fresh fillets (snapper or grouper)
- 1 teaspoon salt, seasoned
- 1 tablespoon fresh juice of a lime
- 1 can of beer or a Greenie is fine

Directions
- Fill deep fryer, or a deep saucepan about 3/4 full with oil or fat for frying. Heat to 375 degrees F.
- Cut fillets into serving size pieces and brush with lime juice.
- In a bowl mix the flour, salt and pepper. Gradually add the beer, beating until the batter is a nice smooth texture.
- Add on a plate the extra flour. Coat each piece of fish with flour and dip it into the batter, coating well.
- Fry the fish for seven or eight minutes, turning only once. Use brown paper or absorbent paper towels to drain the fish on. Serve with cole slaw and fried potatoes.

Crab Chowder with Sherry

Ingredients
- 115 g (4 oz.) Crabmeat
- White part of 1 Leek, finely chopped
- 1 onion, finely chopped
- 1 celery stalk, finely chopped
- 2 ripe tomatoes, peeled, seeded and diced
- 2 tbsp. butter
- 1 liter (4 cups) fish stock or Clam juice
- 4 basil leaves
- 1 tsp. thyme
- 60 ml (1/4 cup) dry sherry
- Salt and pepper

Directions
- Melt the butter in a large saucepan; add the leek, onion and celery; sauté over medium heat for 3 minutes;
- add the tomatoes and continue cooking 3 minutes longer;
- add the fish stock or clam juice; add the crab, basil and thyme; let simmer, covered, for 10 minutes;
- season with salt and pepper;
- place into individual serving bowls and pour in a little dry sherry just at the moment of serving.

Antigua Scallop and King Prawns Salad

Ingredients
- 3/4 cup corn oil
- 2 x whole vanilla beans
- 1/4 cup fresh lemon juice
- 2 cup sweet potato cooked and diced
- 2 x ripe papayas
- 2 x ripe mango
- 12 x PC medium sized scallops
- 8 x each king size shrimp
- 1 tbl olive oil
- 4 cup mesclun or 4 cup gourmet mixed salad greens
- Salt
- Pepper
- Cajun seasoning mix or Creole seasoning mix

Directions
- If time permits, infuse the oil by placing one vanilla bean in the oil, cover and let stand 2 days up to 2 weeks.
- Dry the second vanilla bean and grind in a spice or coffee grinder.
- Split open the vanilla bean and scrape out the pulp into the corn oil.
- In a small bowl, combine the oil and lemon juice. Season with salt and pepper.

- Peel the papaya and mango.
- Dice one-third of each fruit and stir with the sweet potato into the dressing.
- Cut the remaining fruit lengthwise into thin slices. Separate the head portion of the shrimp from the tails.
  Boil the head of the shrimp until red for garnish. Cut the shrimp tails in half lengthwise, remove from shell and discard the vein.
- Season the scallops and shrimp with salt, pepper and Creole seasoning.
- In a large Non stick pan heat the olive oil, add the reserved vanilla bean and sauté the seafood 2-3 minutes on each side until golden.
- Toss the salad greens with 1/2 cup of the dressing. Arrange in center of four plates.
- With a slotted spoon, drain and arrange the fruit and sweet Potato around the salad.
- Add the scallops, shrimp and some slice fruit attractively over the greens.
- Garnish the plate with the shrimp heads and some fresh Herbs if available.

Shrimp Pie

Ingredients
- 2 Medium Pastry Crusts (Or Pie Crusts)
- 1 Pound Shrimp
- 1 Tablespoon Olive Oil
- 1 Medium Onion — Chopped
- 1 Tablespoon Parsley — Chopped
- 1 Can Palm Hearts
- 3 Tablespoons Flour
- 1 Cup Milk
- 1 Can Tomato Paste
- Salt And Pepper — To Taste
- Tabasco Sauce — To Taste

Directions
- Sauté onions and parsley for 10 minutes. Add shrimp and palm hearts.
- Mix flour with milk, pour over shrimp, cook until mixture thickens, add remaining ingredients.
- Pour into pie crust, cover with other pie crust, vent and bake at 400 degrees for 20 minutes or until crust is lightly browned.

Shrimp Moqueca

Ingredients
- 2 Cloves Garlic — Finely Chopped
- 1/2 Teaspoon Salt
- 1 Pound Shrimp
- 1 Lemon Juice
- 2 Tablespoons Vinegar
- 1 Tablespoon Parsley
- 1 Can Tomato Paste
- Pepper — To Taste
- 2 Tablespoons Dende Oil
- 1/2 Cup Coconut Milk

Directions
- Combine garlic, salt and shrimp. Let stand for 15 minutes.
- Combine onion, lemon juice, vinegar, parsley, tomato paste and pepper.
- Mix in dende oil and shrimp mixture. Add coconut milk and bring to a simmer. Cook until shrimp is done and serve over rice.

Shrimp Cuscuz

Ingredients
- 1 Pound Shrimp
- 1 Lemon Lemon Juice
- Salt And Pepper — To Taste
- 3 Tablespoons Olive Oil
- 1 Medium Onion — Chopped
- 1/4 Cup Parsley — Chopped
- 2 Tablespoons Garlic Salt
- 1 Cup Tomato Sauce
- 1 Medium Jalapeno — Chopped

Directions
- mix together shrimp, lemon juice, pepper and salt. Let stand 1 hour. Sauté onion, parsley in oil for 3 minutes, add garlic salt, tomato sauce and pepper, cover and simmer 20 minutes, Add shrimp and simmer until done.
- Serve over rice, cous cous, polenta or potatoes.
- Garnish with either, hard boiled eggs, sliced tomatoes or olives.

Corn And Shrimp Soup

Ingredients
- 1 Pound Shrimp
- 1 Tablespoon Garlic Powder
- 1 Teaspoon Black Pepper
- 1 Teaspoon Salt
- 2 Cups Corn
- 6 Cups Chicken Stock
- 3 Tablespoons Olive Oil
- 1 Large Onion — Chopped

Directions
- Combine shrimp, garlic powder, salt and pepper. Let stand 15 minutes.
- Sauté onion in olive oil for 10 minutes, add corn and stock, simmer 10 minutes.
- Add shrimp mixture. Cook until shrimp are done, about 5 minutes. Serve.

SALADS

Easy Nicoise Salad Recipe

There are many Nicoise recipes out there but this one is the best!

Preparation Time: 15 minutes
Total Time: 15 minutes
  Yield: 4-6 servings

Ingredients

1 lb. boiled potato, sliced

1 cup canned tuna chunks

1 cup green beans, cut into 1-inch pieces

1 cup cherry tomatoes, halved

1 medium white onion, thinly sliced

½ cup black olives

¼ cup capers, rinsed and drained

3 medium hard-boiled eggs, sliced

1 head Romaine lettuce, leaves separated

Balsamic Vinaigrette with Parsley Dressing:

½ cup olive oil

2 Tbsp. balsamic vinegar

2 Tbsp. Dijon mustard

¼ tsp. dried parsley

salt and freshly ground black pepper

Method

1. Whisk together olive oil, balsamic vinegar, Dijon mustard, and parsley in a small glass bowl. Season with salt and pepper, to taste.
2. In a large salad bowl, combine potato, tuna, green beans, cherry tomatoes, white onion, olives, and capers. Toss gently to combine.
3. Transfer salad onto individual plates with lettuce bed. Top with egg slices and drizzle with prepared dressing.

-

Fennel and Shrimp Salad Recipe

This yummy salad recipe with fennel, shrimp, and spinach is very easy to make and will surely satisfy those tummies!

Preparation Time: 15 minutes
Total Time: 15 minutes
Yield: 3-4 servings

Ingredients
1 medium fennel bulb, shredded
10 oz. boiled shrimps, peeled and deveined
2 medium boiled potatoes, sliced
1 medium white onion, thinly sliced
½ cup green olives
4 cups baby spinach

Lemon Mustard with Thyme Dressing:

½ cup olive oil
2 Tbsp. lemon juice

2 Tbsp. Dijon mustard

¼ tsp. dried thyme

salt and freshly ground black pepper

Method
1. Whisk together olive oil, lemon juice, Dijon mustard, and thyme in a small glass bowl. Season with salt and pepper, to taste.
2. In a large salad bowl, combine the fennel bulb, boiled shrimps, boiled potatoes, white onion, green olives, and spinach. Toss to combine.
3. Transfer in individual salad plates and drizzle with prepared dressing.

-

Mediterranean Chicken Salad Recipe

This Mediterranean-inspired salad recipe with chicken with balsamic vinaigrette makes a scrumptious meal for lunch or light dinner.

Preparation Time: 15 minutes
Total Time: 15 minutes
 Yield: 3-4 servings

Ingredients

10 oz. baked chicken, cut into strips

1 cup cherry tomatoes

1 medium cucumber

1 medium red onion, thinly sliced

½ cup black olives, drained

4 cups iceberg lettuce

Balsamic Vinaigrette with Basil Dressing:
- ½ cup olive oil
- 2 Tbsp. balsamic vinegar
  2 tsp. Dijon mustard
- ¼ tsp. dried basil
- salt and freshly ground black pepper

Method
1. Whisk together olive oil, balsamic vinegar, and basil in a small glass bowl. Season with salt and pepper, to taste.
2. In a large salad bowl, combine cherry tomatoes, cucumber, red onion, black olives. Toss to combine.
3. Transfer in individual plates with lettuce bed. Top with chicken strips and drizzle with prepared dressing.
4. Serve and enjoy.

Tuna, Egg and Potato Salad Recipe

This delicious recipe with tuna, potato, and egg is the best way to get your daily dose of healthy carbs, protein, and antioxidants.

Preparation Time: 15 minutes
Total Time: 15 minutes
    Yield: 3-4 servings

Ingredients

1 cup canned tuna chunks

1 cup cherry tomatoes, halved

1 cup green beans, cut into small pieces

1 lb. baby potatoes, unpeeled, boiled

1 medium red onion, thinly sliced

½ cup black olives, drained

2 medium hard-boiled eggs, sliced

1 head Romaine lettuce, leaves separated

Honey Lemon Mustard Dressing:

½ cup olive oil
2 Tbsp. lemon juice
2 tsp. Dijon mustard
2 tsp. honey
¼ tsp. dried sage
salt and freshly ground black pepper

Method

1. Whisk together olive oil, lemon juice, Dijon mustard, honey, and sage in a small glass bowl. Season with salt and pepper, to taste.
2. In a large salad bowl, combine the tuna, cherry tomatoes, green beans, potatoes, red onion, and black olives. Toss gently to combine.
3. Arrange lettuce on a plate to make a bed. Add tuna salad mixture. Top with egg slices. Drizzle with prepared dressing.

Spiral Pasta and Tuna Salad with Olives Recipe

This satisfying pasta salad recipe with tuna and olives is truly packed with nutrients.

Preparation Time: 15 minutes
Total Time: 15 minutes
Yield: 3-4 servings

Ingredients

2 cups cooked spiral pasta

1 cup canned tuna flakes, drained

2 medium ripe tomatoes, diced

4 black olives, thinly sliced

4 green olives, thinly sliced

½ head Romaine lettuce

Lemon Herb Vinaigrette Dressing:

½ cup olive oil

1 Tbsp. lemon juice

1 Tbsp. Dijon mustard

1 Tbsp. fresh mixed herbs, finely chopped
salt and freshly ground black pepper

Method

1. Whisk together olive oil, lemon juice, Dijon mustard, and mixed herbs in a small glass bowl. Season with salt and pepper, to taste.
2. Place the pasta, tuna, tomato, olives, in a large salad bowl. Season with salt and pepper, to taste. Drizzle with prepared lemon herb vinaigrette. Toss to combine.
3. Transfer in serving dish on a bed of lettuce leaves. Garnish with fresh parsley, if desired.
4. Serve and enjoy.

Fresh Summer Fruit Salad

Revitalize your body with this delicious and healthy snack option made from a combination of fresh summer fruits

Preparation Time: 10 minutes
Total Time: 10 minutes
Yield: 4 servings

Ingredients

1 medium apple, cored and cut into small wedges

2 medium kiwifruit, peeled and sliced

8 pcs. strawberries, cleaned and halved

8 pcs. raspberries

1 cup seedless grapes

Method

1. Place all fruits in a medium bowl. Toss to combine.
2. Divide in individual serving cups.
3. Serve and enjoy!

SNACKS

Cucumber and Carrot Sticks in Ranch Dip

A healthy and crunchy snack you can munch on without feeling guilty.

Preparation Time: 10 minutes
Total Time: 20 minutes
Yield: 4 servings

Ingredients

2 medium cucumber, cut into 3-inch sticks
2 medium carrots, cut into 3-inch sticks

Ranch Dip
¼ cup sour cream
¼ cup light mayonnaise
1 ½ tsp. lime juice
1 Tbsp. coriander leaves, chopped
1 Tbsp. chives, chopped

Method
1. In a small mixing bowl, mix together sour cream, mayonnaise, lime juice, coriander and chives. Mix well and store in refrigerator until ready to use.
2. Arrange cucumber and carrots sticks in individual serving cups.
3. Take out chilled ranch dip, and transfer in a serving bowl. Garnish with coriander leaves.
4. Serve and enjoy.

Tomato and Herb Bruschetta

Enjoy this bruschetta made of tomatoes, herbs and wholegrain baguette.

Preparation Time: 15 minutes
Total Time: 15 minutes
Yield: 4 servings

Ingredients

½ loaf wholegrain baguette, sliced into ½-inch thick

3 medium tomatoes, diced

¼ cup fresh basil, chopped

1 tsp. fresh thyme, chopped

1 clove garlic, minced

2 Tbsp. extra virgin olive oil

2 Tbsp. balsamic vinegar

salt and pepper, to taste

Method
1.   In a medium bowl, combine together tomatoes, basil, thyme, and garlic. Drizzle with olive oil and balsamic vinegar. Toss to coat well. Season with salt and pepper, to taste.
2.   Toast baguette slices in a broiler for about 1 minute.
3.   Use a dessert spoon to scoop the tomato mixture over the toasted bread and place on a serving dish. Garnish with fresh basil leaves, if desired.
4.   Serve and enjoy.

Veggies with Garlic Hummus

Tired of ordinary dips? Try out this delicious garlic hummus dip served with veggies.

Preparation Time: 15 minutes
Total Time: 15 minutes

Yield: 4 servings

Ingredients

4 celery stalks, cut into 3-inch inches

1 medium carrot, peeled and cut into 3-inch inches

1 medium red bell pepper, cut into strips

Garlic Hummus Dip

15 oz. canned chickpeas or cooked chickpeas

4 cloves garlic, roasted and chopped

¼ cup olive oil

¼ cup Tahini

¼ tsp. fresh ground pepper

¼ tsp. cumin

2 Tbsp. lemon juice

¼ cup reserved chickpea liquid or water

Salt and lemon pepper, to taste

Method

1. To make the garlic hummus, first peel off all chickpea skins.
2. Put chickpeas in food processor and process for 2-3 minutes or until it has turned into a mashed consistency.
3. Add in the roasted garlic, olive oil, tahini, pepper, cumin, and lemon juice. Process for 1-2 minutes or until creamy in consistency.

4. Gradually pour in the reserved chickpea liquid and process for additional 1 minute. Season with salt and lemon pepper, to taste.
5. Transfer hummus into a serving bowl and drizzle with olive oil.
6. Garnish with minced garlic or paprika, if desired.
7. Serve with veggie sticks on the side.

Pita Chips and Veggies with Hummus

Make your snacks healthier with this delicious pita chips and veggie sticks with Hummus.

Preparation Time: 15 minutes
Total Time: 15 minutes
Yield: 4 servings

Ingredients
2 whole wheat pita bread, cut into 8 triangles, toasted

1 medium carrot, cut into 3-inch sticks

2 celery stalks, cut into 3-inch sticks

Hummus

15 oz. chickpeas

¼ cup lemon juice

¼ cup Tahini

2 ½ Tbsp. water

1 clove garlic, minced

2 Tbsp. olive oil

1 tsp. cumin, ground

1 tsp. paprika, ground

Salt and pepper, to taste

Method

1. Make hummus by combining chickpeas, lemon juice, tahini, water, garlic, oil, cumin, and paprika in a food processor. Process for 1 minute or until mashed and has smooth texture. Season with salt and pepper, to taste. Process for another 30 seconds.
2. If the consistency of the hummus is too thick, gradually add more water into the mixture to attain the desired consistency.
3. Once the desired consistency is achieved, thoroughly scrape the hummus out of the food

processor into a small serving bowl. Drizzle olive oil over the top of the mixture and garnish with paprika.
4. Serve with pita chips and veggie sticks on the side.

Yogurt Cereal and Berry Parfait

A quick and easy yogurt, cereal and berry parfait that is ideal for snack or dessert!

Preparation Time: 15 minutes
Total Time: 15 minutes
Yield: 4 servings

Ingredients

2 cups low-fat yogurt, vanilla

1 cup corn flakes cereal, crushed

4 Tbsp. raspberry syrup

1 cup raspberry, fresh

1 cup blackberries, fresh

Method

1. In a round glass or parfait glass, layer the bottom with yogurt and then followed by the raspberry syrup.
2. Add in crushed corn flakes and berries.
3. Top with another layer of yogurt, cereals, and berries. Cover and chill until ready to serve.
4. Serve and enjoy.

RISOTTOS

Creamy Asparagus Risotto with Parmesan

With this recipe the herbs complements well with the creamy risotto and asparagus.

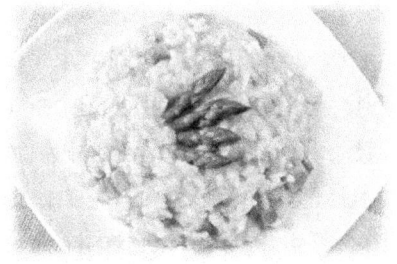

Preparation time: 10 minutes
Total time: 40 minutes
Yield: 4 servings

Ingredients

2 cups reduced sodium chicken stock

2 cups water

2 tablespoons unsalted butter, divided

½ cup shallots

1 cup Arborio rice

¼ cup dry white wine

½ cup half and half cream

½ pound asparagus

½ cup parmesan cheese

freshly ground black pepper

Method
1. Bring chicken stock and water to a boil in a stockpot. Remove from heat.
2. Trim the asparagus, cut off tips and peel the tough skins of the spears.
3. In a saucepan over medium heat, cook 1 tablespoon butter. Add the shallots; cook until translucent for about 1 to 2 minutes. Add the rice, stir until nicely coated. Cook for 2 more minutes.
4. Add the wine. Cook, stirring until the rice absorbs the wine.
5. Add ½ cup of the stock, stirring until the liquid is completely absorbed; add more stock in ½ cup increments at a time. To prevent the rice from sticking to the bottom of the pan, stir often. Cook for about 20 to 25 minutes until the rice is tender but still firm to the bite. Add the asparagus and cream halfway through cooking time. Remove from heat.
6. Stir in the parmesan cheese together with 1 tablespoon butter. Season with pepper to taste.
7. Serve immediately and enjoy.

Easy Seafood Risotto

Delicious and filling, this risotto recipe with crabmeat and shrimp is sure to please!

Preparation time: 10 minutes
Total time: 45 minutes
Yield: 6 servings

Ingredients

3 cups clam juice

2 ½ cups water

2 tablespoons extra-virgin olive oil

1 medium onion, finely chopped

1 ½ cup Arborio rice

½ cup dry white wine

1 tablespoon unsalted butter

½ pound shrimp, cooked, shelled

½ pound lump crab meat

salt and freshly ground pepper

Method
1. Bring clam juice and water to a boil in a medium saucepan over medium-high heat. Remove from heat. Set aside.

2. Heat olive oil in a heavy-bottomed sauce pan. Sauté onion for 1 minute.

3. Add the rice and cook for 2 minutes.

4. Add the wine and cook until it is absorbed by the rice, stirring often.

5. Add ½ cup clam juice at a time stirring frequently until it is nearly absorbed between additions. Cook for 20-25 minutes. Remove from heat.

6. Meanwhile, melt butter in a skillet over medium heat. Cook the shrimp and crab for 3-5 minutes. Combine mixture into the risotto. Mix well. Season with salt and pepper to taste.

7. Transfer to a serving dish.

8. Serve immediately and enjoy.

Pumpkin and Sage Risotto

This risotto recipe is perfect during fall or whenever pumpkins are abundant.

Preparation time: 10 minutes
Total time: 40 minutes
Yield: 4 servings

-

Ingredients

2 cups chicken stock

2 cups water

2 Tbsp. olive oil

1 medium onion, chopped

1 cup Arborio rice

1 lb. pumpkin, diced

½ cup pumpkin puree

2 tablespoons fresh sage leaves

¼ teaspoon cinnamon, ground

¼ teaspoon nutmeg, finely grated

salt and freshly ground black pepper

Method

1. Bring chicken stock and water to a simmer in a pot over medium heat.
2. In a heavy-bottomed saucepan, sauté onion until soft.
3. Add the rice and cook for a couple of minutes to coat the grains with oil.
4. Stir in 1/3 of the stock and bring to a simmer. Add the pumpkin, pumpkin puree, sage, cinnamon, and nutmeg stirring often. Once stock is almost absorbed add more stock one ladleful at a time until rice is al dente and pumpkin is soft, about 20-25 minutes. Season with salt and pepper, to taste. Remove from heat.
5. Transfer to a serving dish.
6. Serve immediately and enjoy.

Risotto with Spinach and Parmesan

This is a no-fuss lunch or dinner recipe. Tasty yet very easy to make!

Preparation time: 10 minutes
Total time: 45 minutes
Yield: 6-8 servings

Ingredients
4 cups vegetable broth, unsalted
2 Tbsp. extra-virgin olive oil
½ cup onion, finely chopped
1 lb. spinach, stemmed and sliced thinly
1 cup Arborio rice
¼ cup dry white wine
2 Tbsp. unsalted butter

¼ cup parmesan cheese, freshly grated
freshly grated nutmeg
salt and freshly ground black pepper

Method

1. Bring vegetable broth to a boil in a pot over medium heat. Remove from heat.

2. In a heavy-bottomed saucepan, sauté onion in olive oil over medium heat until softened.

3. Add the rice and stir until well coated with oil; cook for 2 minutes.

4. Add the wine and stir until absorbed.

5. Add the broth one ladleful at a time, stirring often. Reserve ¼ cup of the broth to add towards the end. Cook rice for about 18 minutes.

6. Add spinach and the reserved ¼ cup of broth. Stir occasionally until spinach mixture is wilted and rice is al dente for about 3-5 minutes. Remove from heat. Stir in

butter, parmesan cheese, and nutmeg. Season with salt and pepper, to taste.

7. Serve immediately and enjoy.

Easy Vegetarian Risotto

This is a great dish that vegetarians will surely enjoy.

Preparation Time: 10 minutes
Total Time: 45 minutes
Yield: 6 servings

Ingredients

6 cups water

1 medium carrot, thinly sliced

1 cup green beans, trimmed and cut into 2-inch pieces

2 cups broccoli, cut into small florets

2 tablespoons olive oil

2 shallots, chopped

1 clove garlic, minced

½ teaspoon fresh ginger, grated

1 ½ cups Arborio rice

½ cup dry white wine

½ cup cheddar cheese, grated

¼ cup fresh chives, chopped

salt and freshly ground black pepper

Method

1. Bring water to a boil in a stockpot over medium heat. Add the vegetables (carrot, green beans, and broccoli); cook for 5-7 minutes. Transfer vegetables to a plate and reserve vegetable stock.
2. In a heavy-bottomed saucepan, sauté shallots, garlic, and ginger in olive oil over medium heat until fragrant.
3. Add the rice and stir until well coated with oil; cook for 2 minutes.
4. Add the wine and stir until absorbed.
5. Add the stock one ladleful at a time, stirring often. Reserve 1/2 cup of the stock to add towards the end. Cook rice for about 18 minutes.
6. Add the vegetables and reserved 1/2 cup of stock. Stir occasionally until rice is al dente for about 3-5 minutes. Remove from heat. Season with salt and pepper, to taste.
7. Transfer to a serving dish. Sprinkle with cheddar cheese and chives.
8. **Serve immediately and enjoy.**

Easy Risotto with Salmon and Zucchini

This wonderful risotto recipe has a lot of healthy components that you need in a meal!

Preparation time: 10 minutes
Total time: 45 minutes
Yield: 6 servings

Ingredients
3 cups vegetable stock
2 cups water
2 tablespoons olive oil
½ cup scallions, chopped
2 cloves garlic, minced
1 ½ cups Arborio rice
½ cup dry white wine
1 medium zucchini, diced
1 cup baked salmon fillet, flaked
½ cup milk

1 tablespoon thyme, chopped
½ teaspoon coriander seed, ground
salt and freshly ground black pepper

-

-

Method
1. Bring vegetable stock and water to a boil in a stockpot over medium heat. Remove from heat.
2. In a heavy-bottomed saucepan, stir-fry scallions and garlic in oil over medium heat until fragrant.
3. Add the rice and stir until well coated with oil; cook for 2 minutes.
4. Add the wine and stir until absorbed.
5. Add the zucchini and vegetable stock one ladleful at a time, stirring often. Cook rice for about 20-25 minutes or until al dente. Adding the salmon, milk, thyme, and coriander towards the last 5 minutes of cooking time. Remove from heat. Season with salt and pepper, to taste.
6. Transfer to a serving dish.
7. Serve immediately and enjoy.

SEAFOOD

Asian Pan Fried Cod with Spring Onions Recipe

This simple yet delectable dish with cod is so easy to cook and only needs few ingredients.

Preparation Time: 10 minutes
Total Time: 25 minutes
Yield: 4 servings

Ingredients

4 (4 oz.) cod fillets

salt and ground black pepper to taste

1 Tbsp. peanut oil

2 Tbsp. butter

2 Tbsp. lemon juice

2 cloves garlic, chopped

¼ cup spring onion

Method

1. Season the cod fillets with salt and pepper on both sides. Set aside.
2. Heat peanut oil in a non-stick pan over medium-high heat. Sear fillets for 2 minutes on each side or until browned. Transfer to a clean plate. Cover with foil to keep warm.
3. Using the same pan, melt butter over medium-high heat. Stir-fry garlic until aromatic, about 1 minute. Stir in lemon juice and cook further 1 minute.
4. Add the fish fillets and cook for 2 minutes on each side.
5. Transfer to a serving platter. Drizzle with lemon-butter sauce from the pan. Sprinkle with spring onion.
6. Serve immediately and enjoy.

Homemade Chili Garlic Prawns Recipe

This spicy seafood recipe with prawns, chili, and garlic makes a delicious appetizer or dinner. Just serve with rice and steamed broccoli to have a complete meal.

Preparation Time: 10 minutes
Total Time: 20 minutes
Yield: 6-8 servings

Ingredients

3 Tbsp. butter, chopped

1 Tbsp. olive oil

3 garlic cloves, thinly sliced

1 tsp. cayenne pepper

2 lbs. medium king prawns, peeled, deveined, tails intact

1 Tbsp. tomato paste

Steamed broccoli, to serve

Method
1. In a skillet or non-stick pan, heat butter and oil over medium-high heat. Stir-fry garlic and chilli. Cook for 1 minute or until aromatic.
2. Add the prawns. Cook, stirring for 2 to 3 minutes or until prawns turned pink.
3. Stir in tomato paste.
4. Serve with steamed broccoli and enjoy.

Asian-Style Shrimp and Vegetable Sauté Recipe

<u>This healthy seafood recipe has the perfect blend of flavors and nutrients from the shrimps, carrots, and snow peas.</u>

Preparation Time: 15 minutes
Total Time: 15 minutes
Yield: 3-4 servings

Ingredients

1 Tbsp. olive oil

1 medium onion, chopped

2 cloves garlic, minced

1 lb. fresh shrimps, peeled and deveined

1 lb. carrots, julienned (cut into thin strips)

2 cups snow peas or snap peas

salt and freshly ground black pepper

Method
1. Heat oil in a large skillet over medium-high heat. Stir-fry onion and garlic for 1-2 minutes or until fragrant.
2. Add the shrimps, carrot, and snow peas. Cook, stirring for 5-7 minutes. Season with salt and pepper, to taste. Remove from heat.
3. Transfer to a serving dish.
4. Serve and enjoy.

-

Breaded Fish Fillet Recipe

Quick and easy fish recipe, even people who aren't fond of eating fish will love these crispy fillets!

Preparation Time: 20 minutes
Total Time: 20 minutes
Yield: 4 servings

Ingredients

4 (4 oz.) fillets sole

1 whole egg

2 Tbsp. prepared yellow mustard

½ tsp. salt

1 cups panko (breadcrumbs)

¼ cup vegetable oil, for frying

Method

1. In a shallow bowl, whisk together egg, and yellow mustard. Season with salt and pepper, to taste. Set aside.
2. Place the panko in another shallow bowl.
3. Heat oil in a large skillet or non-stick fry pan over medium-high heat.
4. Dip each fish fillets in egg-mustard mixture. Dredge the fillets in panko, making sure to fully coat the fish.
5. Cook fish fillets in hot oil for 3-4 minutes on each side, or until golden brown.
6. Serve with your choice of dip and enjoy.

Grilled Scallops with Teriyaki Sauce Recipe

This Asian-inspired seafood dish only requires a few ingredients yet packed with flavor.

Preparation Time: 15 minutes
Total Time: 1 hour 15 minutes
Yield: 3-4 servings

Ingredients

1 lb. dry sea scallops

¼ cup Teriyaki sauce

2 cloves garlic, minced

¼ tsp. freshly ground black pepper

wooden skewers

Method

8. Place the scallops, Teriyaki sauce, garlic, and pepper in a zip lock bag. Shake to combine. Refrigerate for at least an hour.
9. Preheat grill to high.
10. Thread the scallops onto wooden skewers. Grill for 3-4 minutes on each side.
11. Transfer in serving dish.
12. Serve and enjoy.

www.ingramcontent.com/pod-product-compliance
Lightning Source LLC
Chambersburg PA
CBHW071438070526
44578CB00001B/128